Material Transfers

Metaphor, Craft, and Place in
Contemporary Architecture

Françoise Astorg Bollack

Material Transfers

Metaphor, Craft, and Place in Contemporary Architecture

The Monacelli Press

For Tom Killian

First published in the United States by The
Monacelli Press. All rights reserved.

Library of Congress Control Number
2020941166
ISBN 978-158093-5432

Design: Shawn Hazen, hazencreative.com

Printed in China

The Monacelli Press
65 Bleecker Street
New York, New York 10012

Photography Credits:

Matthew Blunderfield 83, 87
Roberto Conto for Edoardo Tesoldi 72–79
Tim Crocker 148–54
Michael Middleton Dwyer 23
Michel Denance 162–69
Getty Images 18, 82
Courtesy of Kengo Kuma & Associates 43–49
Jens Marcus Linde 50–57
Y. Marchand and R. Meffe 154–61
Courtesy of Marx & Sketetee Architects 96–101
Ximo Michavila 88–95
Adam Mork 102–107
James Morris 34–41
Stefan Muller 58–65
Courtesy of Pollard, Thomas, Edwards Architects 126–31
Philippe Ruault 118–25
Daria Scagliola and Stijn Brakee for MVRDV 132–47
Celia Uhalde 162–69

Contents

Introduction

"Without change, there is no history, without regularity there is no time."[1]

AFTER ALMOST A century of unchecked belief in the superior value of "the new" and the universal validity of modern forms, we continue to rediscover the richness of our existing built environment and what it has to teach us. Since the mid-1960s, we have been inventing design strategies that relate to existing building patterns rather than break from them. This is an ongoing project, a work in progress; as architects redefine the meaning of contextual design, this endeavor has enormous consequences for the preservation of our built world since new buildings can support it or undermine it, add or detract, depending on their attitude. As we continue to deepen our appreciation of historical models, I believe that it is now time to look at the possibilities of design strategies using metaphor, mimesis, and modern building craft to help us inhabit, once again, specific places. This is what this book is about.

In 1931 William Harlan Hale, one of the editors of *The Harkness Hoot*, wrote: "No man and no nation who possessed a life-giving creative sense ever dreamed of copying the previous age. We associate the phenomenon of imitation with people who are sterile, with eras whose tendency is retrogression and atavism."[2] The article coincided with the opening of the Sterling Memorial Library at Yale University designed by James Gamble Rogers. Hale was hardly alone in his negative view of a contemporary architecture that was seen as imitative and not Modern with an uppercase M. We have continued to conflate imitation and copy, relegating both to the special hell inhabited by those who are on the wrong side of history. Indeed, the Collegiate Gothic style of the Sterling Memorial Library and of the Yale campus as a whole, and all such design procedures, were roundly rejected by modernist architects not only as unsuited to our highly evolved lifestyle and modern sensibility but also as morally corrupt because they involved copying, duplicating, or imitating earlier models—no matter how inventive these new designs often were.

Today, visitors walking through the gates of many American colleges and universities—Bryn Mawr, Yale, Princeton, and others—enjoy the comfort of a familiar environment. The stone buildings, the steeply pitched slate roofs with their massive chimneys, the small-paned casement windows are all familiar and unquestioned. Not only is this environment associated with prestigious institutions of learning, but it also evokes— as it was meant to do—older, cherished images of Oxford and Cambridge, and, beyond that, images of medieval religious architecture with their rich associations. The difference between the earlier historicist approach to copying and our own contemporary approach is the advent of modern art and the advent of conceptual art. We now see copying in very different terms. We have recuperated it as a dare and as a provocative procedure, and therefore this process is in the foreground; we do it as an iconoclastic act, an act of defiance, so the procedure itself becomes the subject of the work, while, at the same time, the design concerns iteslf with establishing a continuity with what exists.

According to the art historian George Kubler, "Human desires in every present instant are torn between the replica and the invention, between the desire to return to the known pattern, and the desire to escape it by a new variation" and "No act ever is completely novel, and no act can ever be quite accomplished without variation."[3] The Dutch architectural firm MVRDV asserts that "copies continue a sequence unraveled by the prime object. But they also prove that formal sequences exceed the ability of any individual creation to exhaust its own possibilities."[4] That Kubler was writing in 1962 and MVRDV published *Copy Paste* in 2017 demonstrates the continued relevance of this topic.

At the present moment, might we not reconsider the act of imitation in architecture—mimesis, duplication, replication—in a new way? Scrubbed of its spurious, and outdated, moral opprobrium, could it have something to offer to contemporary architectural practice? Could it unlock new possibilities when we build in existing contexts? Could it provide new ways to move forward while holding on to what we have?

When designing new buildings or additions in existing contexts, architects are confronted with the need to propose buildings that "fit in," while they also feel a need to stand out, to experiment, and to do something new. These contradictory pressures create a fertile climate for the development of new strategies. The new buildings that are designed and built in an attempt to resolve this conundrum cannot be characterized as part of a movement or as being in "a style," but they are part of a developing body of work experimenting with architectural strategies such as mimesis or replication, and new craft practices of unorthodox coupling of material and combination of materials and form, all of which challenge modern architecture's taboos. The relationship between metaphor, materials, and craft is being tested and restated.

One of the questions to be answered is how we should respond to the world as it is, how we should intervene in an increasingly dense and increasingly managed environment. The *tabula rasa* favored by many theories of modern architecture is unsatisfactory, and we have come to see value in certain forms of historical and architectural continuity. But how and where are we to find this continuity? Are we to find it in building forms, in the long-remembered and familiar forms of our building culture, the champions (in a medieval sense) of successive cultural expressions and architectural sensibilities—house forms, temple forms, and so on— and can we find comfort in metaphorical evocations of these forms? Are we to satisfy this longing for continuity by a renewed attention to materials and craft, the rich, dense archive of our culture? But, at the same time, where are we to find a fresh place for "the new" within the constraints of this longed-for continuity?

How should we satisfy the need and the desire to incorporate traditional forms and elements of memory within an ethos that continues to privilege invention and newness (notions at times limited to a reductive interpretation of innovation). Many modern architects and artists claimed that we had reached "the end of history." That period, with its mindset, is over, but we retain a lingering sense of unease when considering the use of premodern historical forms because we have absorbed a belief in the morality of the "truth of materials," the belief that there is a direct, necessary, and truthful connection between a material and the forms that it makes possible. If this truthful connection exists, it would preclude the use of modern materials in the construction of traditional forms. Louis Kahn's statement about the essential relationship between "the brick" and "the arch" summarizes this attitude: "The brick wants to become an arch"[5] Never mind that Thomas L. Schumacher quipped that when the brick was asked what it wanted to be, the brick (probably remembering its Roman past) said: "I want to be covered with marble," a perfect postmodern statement.

There is now a domain of architectural practice where architects are experimenting with the relationship of form and materials. At first glance the form is recognizable; our eyes and brain tell us that what we are seeing is familiar. Feelings of comfort and nostalgia take over, and we almost forget to look further. Then we realize that this familiar form is built in an unfamiliar material, and we stop to ponder. This recognizable form, often simplified, is not associated with a particular architect; it is an archetype, an "ideal" functioning as a cultural myth, which then becomes available for various overlays. To quote the artist Richard Prince about advertising images (which I equate with "familiar forms"): "Advertising images aren't associated with an author, they look like they have no history to them—like they showed up all at once. They look like what art always wants to look like."

Architects then appropriate a familiar form—whatever it is in a particular instance—and reproduce it, redesign it, with materials unfamiliar to it. Questions arise about how much or how little the new work will try to replicate the source image and about the procedures of this mimesis. The new work finds itself "poised on the knife-edge between the nineteenth-century tradition of copying and the modern strategy of originality."[6]

With the projects included in this book, originality and invention can often be found in sophisticated and intensive material research focused either on reproduction or evocation of the original form's materials and of its construction or on translation and at times reversal of the original form's material qualities. This is all a rich stew of hands-on, trial-and-error research, collaboration between architects, manufacturers and craftspeople, the expansion of traditional techniques, up-to-the-moment digital procedures (as when the architect's digital files are used by the manufacturer's CNC[7] machines) and white-coat laboratory research.

The use of "modern" materials to construct historical forms may be a way to appropriate familiar historical forms, which have almost achieved the dimension of myths, and to reintegrate them into a modern practice through a set of transfers involving metaphor and craft. In other words, two elements are being reconsidered: the traditional form and its materials. The relationship of one to the other, which we thought was immutable, is dissolved; different materials and different construction methods are used to build the "old" form, which becomes transformed and rejuvenated. Society (clients, architectural critics, neighbors) is an agent in this process so that the new procedures, which cannot be ignored, become part of a broader cultural dialogue between the old and the new. The new procedures can be either endorsed or opposed, but in either case, the new work poses the question of the relationship of the new to the old and what, in the end, the new might consist of.

This book examines projects that experiment with this "de-coupling" of form and materials, under the positive pressure of place and context, and suggests what we can learn from these discoveries. Why do this in the first place? What results from this transference? What becomes of the relationship of form to content, of form to representation, of form to construction? What is the nature of the architectural "invention"? Is this practice a direct result of the increasing number of protected heritage areas and buildings? Is it a rebellion against the tyranny of "the new" as, in the words of Robert Rauschenberg, "Having to be different is the same trap as having to be the same."[8] Is it a way for us to establish a different relationship between our contemporary production and historical precedents? Ultimately, how do we extract some general thoughts about the benefits—or dangers—of these strategies?

I believe that this kind of experimentation should be understood in the context of the postmodern drive to come to terms with the role of historic forms in contemporary architecture and with the continued validity of the traditional models. My previous book, *Old Buildings/New Forms: New Directions in Architectural Transformations*, examined the concept-driven approach favored by architects who are seeking to relate to history and an existing context but to do so within the modern ethos. A conceptual approach is also at the basis of the buildings being examined here; in this case, it consists of the use of recognizable metaphors and experimentation with materials, and their craft.

This strategy of appropriation, duplication, repetition, and material transfers (with the resultant shifts in expression) has parallels in our contemporary visual arts culture. The Museum of Modern Art defines appropriation as "the intentional borrowing, copying, and alteration of existing images and objects. A strategy that has been used by artists for millennia, it took on new significance in the mid-twentieth century with the rise of consumerism and the proliferation of images through mass media outlets from magazines to television."[9]

If we believe with the sociologist Gabriel Tarde that a social group is "a collection of beings as long as they are in the process of imitating each other or as long as, without imitating themselves in fact, they resemble each other and that their common characteristics are ancient copies of a same model,"[10] then imitation is the social practice that holds a "collection of beings" together it is the binder that gives cohesion to a social group. Thus, the common, and often unconscious, process of imitation of a common model is critical to social cohesion and to social experience.

As Rosalind Krauss has written about the work of Sherri Levine whose work appropriates known existing images," This is a complex of cultural practices, among them a demythologizing criticism and a truly postmodernist art, both of them acting now to void the basic propositions of modernism, to liquidate them by exposing their fictitious condition. It is thus from a strange new perspective that we look back on the modernist origin and watch it splinter into endless replication."[11]

One only needs to think of the *Double Elvis* by Andy Warhol, where one image is a duplication of the other, or of *Drowning Girl* by Roy Lichtenstein, which is a copy (almost) of *Run for Love*, a D.C. Comics cover, or of *Giant Soft Fan* by Claes Oldenburg, where a table fan, its cord, and plug are reproduced in a limp vinyl material, or of *Pencil* and *Pink Pearl Eraser* by Vija Celmins, works that faithfully reproduce these familiar desk objects at a larger scale and in a different material, or more recently, of *Looking Toward the Avenue* by Jim Dine, which reproduces the *Venus de Milo* in bronze and then presents three of them in different sizes (14, 18, and 23 feet high) on Sixth Avenue in New York. And then there are artists like Cey Adams who painstakingly reproduce well known commercial images, "brands," in different media.

There is a considerable critical literature and a lively, ongoing debate about duplication, imitation, copying as these procedures relate to the visual arts, but there is very little discussion of this phenomenon in architecture. In particular, Andy Warhol's work has been the subject of intense reflection:

> Gerhard Richter and Andy Warhol, whose significant transformations of the source image (cropping, enlarging, reframing) and translation into a different medium have the effect of emancipating the borrowing from its original context, while keeping its distance from its new setting, allowing the image to retain an autonomy and authority, free from the imputation of authorial control. This suspension of artistic intention is aided and abetted by the use of photo-mechanical means of production such as silk screening, into which Warhol has allowed imperfections and accidents to creep in, lending the mechanical and non-descript look of the model its appearance of mechanical reproducibility.[12]

When Roy Lichtenstein produced *Drowning Girl* and Andy Warhol painted *Double Elvis,* these were a pot of paint thrown in the face of the art establishment. These acts put into question the accepted definition of the author, the definition of originality and innovation, the definition of what a legitimate work of art (to say nothing of where the notion of "art" might be located), and most importantly the relevance of the division between high art and "low" art.

The long shadow of the modern movement's astringent theories has kept architects from availing themselves of the freedom from tired old clichés, a freedom that artists claimed so spectacularly for their work in the middle of the twentieth century, but the projects featured here begin to open the door and to shift the discourse's center of gravity towards a more inclusive view of what "making" is about, what architecture is, and what its relationship to the existing built world could be, today.

Remembered Forms
New Materials

IN THE HISTORY of architecture, there are specific moments when the practice of imitation has gone hand in hand with the emergence of a new direction. In these instances, the design replicates an older form but transfers it into a different set of materials to produce something new. Kenneth Frampton has noted: "As Semper was to point out in his Stoffwechseltheorie, the history of culture manifests occasional transpositions in which the architectonic attributes of one mode are expressed in another for the sake of retaining traditional symbolic value, as in the case of the Greek temple, where stone is cut and laid in such a way as to reinterpret the form of the archetypal timber frame."[1] That a new work could result from copying and that this new work could be materially and aesthetically independent of its source is worth noting, while, at the same time, it is worth keeping in mind that the new work could not exist without the source image. It is this ambiguity that allows for innovation and continuity at the same time.

What do I mean by "material transfer"? The model could be imitated, and the imitation could be constructed in materials similar to the model. This is what happened when Henry Flitcroft (1697–1769) designed the Pantheon at Stourhead and when Lord Burlington (1694–1753) designed Chiswick House, both based on Palladio's Villa Rotonda, itself a distant imitation of the Pantheon in Rome. None of the "copies" are exact imitations of the source building and the materials of the mimetic buildings are not the same, but the changes in materials do not appear to be at the heart of the matter. These are all important buildings in the history of architecture, and the fact that they imitated an earlier building, and how they did it, is part of their significance as it is this very act that pointed to new directions in architecture.

Conversely, the facade of the church of Santa Maria Novella, as completed by Leone Battista Alberti offers us, on the upper part (the lower part of the facade was existing), a two-dimensional, idealized copy of a Roman temple front. The materials and the construction of this facade are not at all as they would have been in the Roman temple: the facade is almost totally flat, and the pilasters do not support the entablature or the pediment. They are just thin slabs of marble, a cladding anchored to the back-up brick wall, not load-bearing elements in a trabeated system as they would have been in a Roman temple.

Greek Revival architecture produced beautiful buildings in the late eighteenth and the nineteenth century, and many were monumental public buildings built of load-bearing masonry. When the classical masonry language of temple construction was transferred to wood construction built by carpenters, as it was in northern Europe and the United States, it underwent an extraordinary evolution. It continued to be indebted to the classical models, and at the same time it was liberated from strict adherence to its sources and produced a rich vernacular. This is true as well of the Gothic Revival as it developed in the United States: the shift in materials, from stone to painted wood became the source of the formal inventiveness visible in so many buildings.

In the late nineteenth century, the use of cast iron in construction allowed architects and builders to mine historical styles for the design of their building facades. Palladian and Gothic arches proliferated, and stone quoins, rustications, and fancy stone tooling were replicated in iron cast from molds that could be reused almost infinitely. The cast iron was often painted the color of stone to complete the illusion that these were stone buildings. Hidden in plain sight behind the imitative strategies was an invention: modularity, which became an important compositional device of modern architecture. Philip Johnson wrote about James Bogardus (1800–1874), the inventor and builder who popularized cast-iron architecture along with Daniel Badger: "With the cast-iron facades, he acquainted Americans with modular rhythm, which is the basis of modern design."[2]

What these examples have in common is a process by which an earlier architectural expression was imitated using different materials and different construction methods: from post and lintel construction to thin cladding in the case of Santa Maria Novella, from load-bearing masonry to joined carpentry in the case of Greek and Gothic Revival buildings and from load-bearing masonry to the curtain wall in the case of cast-iron architecture. The material transfers, and the metaphors they served, generated a profound transformation in architecture: it is as if the new developments were made possible by the familiarity of the sources. Except in the case of Santa Maria Novella, imitation and the material shifts that supported it were part of a process that made a high style available to "own" and to build for a large segment of society regardless of means or social status: owners, builders, architects. One of the consequences was an explosion of fresh and inventive vernacular architecture accompanied by a revitalization of the source image. As George Kubler observed: "The replication that fills history actually prolongs the stability of many past moments, allowing sense and pattern to emerge for us wherever we look."[3]

Santa Maria Novella

Florence, Italy

c. 1456–70

Leone Battista Alberti

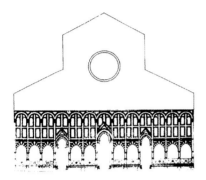

Top: Sketch of the facade before Alberti's intervention.

Above: San Miniato al Monte, Florence, Italy, 1070–1090.

The church of Santa Maria Novella has been extensively discussed in books about the Italian Renaissance. The facade we see today was built in three campaigns over a period of two centuries (c. 1300–c. 1500); the third (1456–1470), attributed to Leone Battista Alberti[4], completed the top half, giving the building its definitive appearance.

At the beginning of this third campaign, the architect was faced with a rough brick wall whose two-tier lower area had been reveted with marble in a contrasting pattern of green and white; the lower tier incorporated ten tombs for the church's patrons, each nested in a deep alcove under a gothic arch. The tombs were integrated in a regular pattern of tall blind arches framing rectangular panels that stretched to the top of the lower facade. In contrast to the Baptistery of San Giovanni (1059–1128) or San Miniato al Monte (started c. 1070/1090 and completed in the early twelfth century) where the arches have depth, at Santa Maria Novella, the architectural pattern is flush, rendered in two dimensions, with the marble cladding treated as a drawing with contrasting green and white marble. The upper facade had been an unfinished brick wall, with a center oculus, closing off the end of the tall nave and the lower side aisles.

Alberti's design, executed between 1456 and 1470, monumentalizes the lower facade by introducing a giant order as a base for the upper facade:

Above: Baptistery of San Giovanni, Florence, Italy, c. 1059–1128.

Below: Upper facade of Santa Maria Novella as designed by Alberti.

the tombs at the extreme left and right are eliminated as are the ones on each side of the new tall center arch. In front of the older facade, the architect adds a giant order consisting of deep framing piers at the sides and four tall columns, all supporting a new plinth at the top of the existing row of blind arches.

The design for the upper elevation is a manifesto, an affirmation of the value of the classical temple model. This new facade is literally a drawing of a prostyle, tetrastyle temple, buttressed by monumental scrolls and crowned by a triangular pediment. Shallow pilasters rest on the new plinth, which provides a strong unifying base and acts as a transition to the building below. This new upper facade is flat except for the depth of the pediment and the depth of the oculus in the center bay of the temple's portico.

This design has usually been discussed in terms of its ideal proportions. Rudolf Wittkower, in his *Architectural Principles in the Age of Humanism*,[5] focuses on the series of squares that provide regulating lines for the organization and on Alberti's proportional system. The new facade is traditionally understood as an exercise in composition, not as a transformative use of representation. As Wittkower notes, "Thus the whole facade is geometrically built up of a progressive duplication or, alternatively, a progressive halving of ratios."[6]

While there is indeed a proportional system embedded in the design, its representational aspects are ground-breaking and unique. This almost two-dimensional drawing of a Roman temple becomes a new building. It is a representation of a Roman temple without any suggestion of depth, a Roman temple re-created as wall architecture. This model to which Renaissance architects aspired is used literally to create new architecture. The image of the old becomes the new, not a re-creation of the model but a memento, an aide memoire, a picture of it, and, in the end, a new thing. This temple is not a temple; it is not a building. It has no depth. No one enters through the center bay. The pilasters, symbolic rather than structural, have almost no depth; their flat rustications executed in green and white have no model in classical architecture.[7] This is not a building meant to be used; it is an ideal to be aspired to, an idea, a sign. It points to the path forward through a process of imitation and transfer. Wittkower has observed that "despite the fact that Alberti intended to reconcile the past and the present, he created the most important facade of the new style and set the example, as is well known, for the most common type of church facade for a long time to come."[8]

Greek Revival

The Doric order, illustrated in *The American Builder's Companion or, A System of Architecture Particularly Adapted to the Present Style of Building.*

The Greek Revival mode in architecture, mostly initiated by the rediscovery of the Greek Doric temples in the middle of the eighteenth century, quickly spread through western, northern and eastern Europe. It suited the new sensibility of the Enlightenment and "was more in harmony with the intellectual requirements of modern culture, which preferred criticism to authority, logic to rhetoric, truth to suggestion, demonstration to persuasion. The point of departure in this turning towards Greece was the Doric order."[9]

The Greek temples at Paestum, which inspired architects in the late eighteenth and early nineteenth century, were massive stone buildings whose impact depended on their weight and their ponderous connection to the earth; the columns supporting the architrave and the roof were either monolithic or built of successive drums anchored on top of each other. This was an architecture of permanence and mass, and it was, for architects and cognoscenti, a link to the golden age of the ancient world.

As the new style imitated and replicated Greek models, it spread through Europe and underwent important material transformations due to differences in culture and construction traditions. In northern Europe in particular, the tradition of wood construction changed the Greek language of stone and mass to one of wood cladding and wood framing while

Above: Moisio Manor summer house, Elimäki, Finland, Carl Ludwig Engel, c. 1830. A good example of the use of the Doric order in a hybrid composition.

Below: The porch of a nineteenth-century house in Mohawk, New York, incorporates a grand Doric order and a vestigial pediment indicating the entrance door.

retaining the authority of the antique through the use of Greek forms, the Doric order in particular.

In the Moisio Manor summer house, for example, the Doric order is used for a porch, appended asymmetrically to a truncated traditional house form in a willful, and prescient, collage of the monumental and the vernacular; the building was designed by Carl Ludwig Engel (1778–1840), who also designed the monumental center of Helsinki. The house is constructed with a log framework structure, faced with horizontal wood boards. The frieze of the semi-circular Doric porch wraps around the traditional house, but in a minor key as the wreaths have been omitted. The exterior wood surface is painted gray to look like stone, and the wood cladding is constructed to mimic rustication; the interior is yellow, and the doors and benches on the porch are brown. The use of color is meaningful in this transfer of a major monumental style, with its implied adherence to a set of fixed standards, to a flexible, endlessly creative vernacular language.

In the United States, this new manner spread through the diffusion of expensive folios accessible to gentlemen amateurs such as Thomas Jefferson (especially from Wood and Dawkins' *Palmyra* and *Baalbek*,[10] which were popular in France), but also through the builders' handbooks widely used by carpenters such as *The Architect or the Practical House Carpenter* (1830), *The Practice of Architecture* (1833), *The Builder's Guide*, (1839), all by Asher Benjamin (1773–1845), and *The Modern Builder's Guide* by Minard Lafever (1798–1854), published in 1833. These guides provided a wealth of models, from instructions on the proper profiles of the classical orders to fully realized designs, all executed in wood. An architecture of stone and mass—and seemingly fixed rules—was then transformed into an architecture of wood framing and painted wood cladding and eventually enriched by vernacular inventions accessible to all. Even Thomas Jefferson's architecture, inspired as it was from Palladian handbooks and new publications on the latest archaeological excavations, is an architecture built of craft materials of wood and brick.

As the historian Dora Wiebenson has observed,

The Greek Revival style suggested a sanctification of civic function, a moral purpose to everyday life—in banks, treasuries, offices, and other commercial buildings. But although civic architecture would be profoundly affected by the first national style, the most enduring and characteristically American architecture was achieved in house design. The colonnade of the classical temple was ideally suited for

Below: Thirteenth Street Presbyterian Church, New York, attributed to Samuel Thomson, 1847.

Bottom: Seneca County courthouse complex in Ovid, New York, 1845–62.

use as the typically and fundamentally American verandah, and it also suggests its forerunner, the Anglo-Palladian *loggia*. It was in this context that the colonnade associated with Greek Revival architecture would appear in domestic architecture.[11]

The development of a domestic vernacular architecture based on Greek models in Europe and in the United States in the first half of the nineteenth century was made possible by the transfer of construction method from stone masonry to wood carpentry. This opened a vast array of possibilities because the carpenter builders and their clients would copy, adapt, and transform what they saw in the handbooks, interpreting the models with great freedom and invention—a freedom that was made possible because, while the style was foreign, the construction methods were thoroughly familiar.

As a result, architectural expressions range from grand and correct to fanciful creations full of inventive deviations.

Portico Place in Manhattan, built as the 13th Street Presbyterian Church in 1847, and attributed to Samuel Thomson, is based on the Theseion in Athens. It is a grand rendition of a Greek temple portico with entablature and pediment. "The Greek Revival style suggested a sanctification of civic function, a moral purpose to everyday life"[12] and this monumental mode is perfectly suited to such a church building (ironically it was converted to apartments in 1982 by Steven B. Jacobs Architect).

This "sanctification of public function" is what inspired the design of the three buildings forming the civic center in Ovid, New York, affectionately

Above left: Cottages, Red Bank, New Jersey.

Above right: Greek Revival garage, Maine.

named "the three bears" or "papa bear, mama bear and baby bear" a friendly acropolis of three temple fronted buildings built between 1845 ("papa bear" as the Ovid County courthouse and "baby bear" as the clerk's office) and 1859–1862 ("mama bear" a new clerk's office built in between the two older buildings). The three buildings consist of a tetrastyle wood portico, in the Doric order in front of a plain brick building.

At the other end of the scale we have three modest cottages in Red Bank, New Jersey, which use the most attenuated classical order for columns that frame a small porch and the correct roof slope—in all a very minimal rendition of distant models. Yet through their frontal presentation, repetition, proportions, and simplicity the buildings achieve a moving dignity.

But in other examples, the carpenter builders used various elements—column, pediment, porch—freely and recomposed them with inexhaustible verve and invention.

In a small garage in Maine, a pediment and an entablature consisting solely of spaced vertical triglyphs, rest on two unfluted corner pilasters with minimal capitals that frame two doors in a wall made of lapped horizontal wood siding.

In the Wadsworth Stable in New Lebanon, Connecticut, c. 1820, the main facade is an assemblage of a grand center made of four shallow pilasters and wings, which exhibit a Palladian arch, with wood keystone, in a rectangular frame. Above this Palladian inspired design is a Greek Revival parapet with a raised center. All the elements are made of wood, the main body of the wall being constructed of flush horizontal boards. The side facade consists of three bays framed by shallow wood pilasters carrying an unadorned entablature. Here we can see that the front and back facades

Above: Wadsworth Stable, Lebanon, Connecticut, c. 1820.

Below: Presbyterian Church, Bedford, New York, 1872. The spires allude to Chartres cathedral, where the spires were built at the different times and vary in height and style.

are simply "false fronts" that hide the slope of the roof in the side bays. The side facade is informal without a dominating symmetrical arrangement and ad hoc accommodations such as the third window from the left cutting through the second pilaster.

Carpenter Gothic

The Gothic Revival style used for churches and other institutions during the nineteenth century was executed in stone, as Gothic cathedrals had been, but in North America, when carpenters built houses, farm buildings, and churches in that style, they transferred the forms of carved stone and load-bearing masonry into a rich vernacular in wood, which came to be called, appropriately, carpenter Gothic. This new manner was inspired by the works and publications of Alexander Jackson Davis and of Andrew Jackson Downing.

Lancet windows, which were structural elements in the original stone models, were replicated in wood even though there was no relationship between the arched form and the structural requirements of wood construction.

Similarly, buttresses were sometimes replicated in small churches simply to reproduce the familiar form of twelfth- and thirteenth-century churches with their great stone flying buttresses. This material transference was supported by new woodworking technology. Steam-powered sawmills provided ample materials for vertical board and batten siding, and new types of saws could cut complex ornament more easily. The development of balloon framing, which produced thinner and lighter walls, allowed more flexibility in design and the remembered Gothic forms were freely recombined and assembled in new arrangements, all executed in wood.

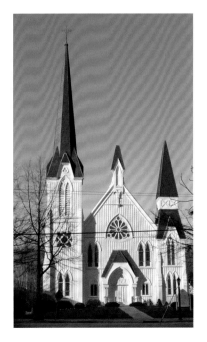

Gothic churches, the source buildings for carpenter Gothic, were built over long periods of time; as buildings progressed, taste and architectural expression changed, and the buildings' form and manner also changed. For example, the west facade of Chartres Cathedral, built between 1194 and 1220, is framed by two towers of quite different height and different design.

In the nineteenth century, builders of carpenter Gothic churches tried to replicate the source buildings, including their odd irregularities. The 1872 Presbyterian Church in Bedford, New York, is a perfect example of this process; while repetitive Gothic element such as flying buttresses, rose windows, lancet windows are used throughout, the two towers on the main facade are deliberately uneven. The painted wood board and batten siding gives this building, as all carpenter Gothic buildings, a quality very different from that of the source buildings—an almost domestic feeling resulting from the fine, even, soft, texture of the vertical painted wood siding. This is a lightweight architecture of wood framing and cladding, an architecture of surface, not an architecture of mass and weight.

It is in the smaller buildings where the builders deployed familiar Gothic elements over simple geometric facades that this new architecture is most compelling. Rose windows, lancet windows, quatrefoil openings, pointed arches, and flying buttresses are arranged in inventive new compositions.

Above: Saint Andrew's Episcopal Church, Prairieville, Alabama, attributed to Richard Upjohn, 1853–54. Note the wood-clad "flying buttresses" on both facades.

Below left: Saint Mary's Chapel, Raleigh, North Carolina, 1855.

Below middle and right: Trinity Parish Chapel, Southport, Connecticut, Disbrow and Taylor, 1871–72.

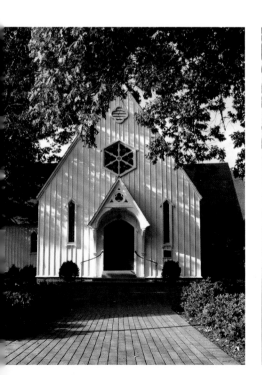

Rose Hill, Bluffton, South Carolina, 1858

Having thus staked their claim for kinship with Gothic architecture, the builders invented new forms, connected to their sources, yes, but also quite modern in their geometric simplicity.

Saint Mary's chapel in Raleigh, North Carolina, 1855–57, is a beautiful example of this approach: a simple gable form facade, clad in board-and-batten siding, on which a small number of elements tell the Gothic story: two tall lancet windows and one rose window with a small quatrefoil opening above it; the entrance door is under a pointed arch and is sheltered by a shallow porch adorned with a small trefoil window. The strategy remains the same even when the design is more complex, as in the Trinity Parish Chapel in Southport, Connecticut, designed by Disbrow and Taylor in 1871. Here there are two nested gable shapes, with vestigial flying buttresses, quatrefoil windows, pointed arches, lancet windows, and of course board-and-batten siding.

Builders also used the coded language of Gothic architecture for residential buildings like Rose Hill Mansion, built in 1858 in Bluffton, South Carolina. Here the abundance and scale of Gothic elements and their repetition conveys opulence rather than the restraint fitting for the design of small churches.

The carpenters who designed and built these buildings were appropriating the high style of historic monumental institutional buildings, and their new modest buildings benefitted from the dignity and authority conferred by the high-style models. On this familiar canvas, they became free to invent, improvise and add endless elaborations, creating an architectural language that was, in the end, quite removed from its Gothic models—an invention, independent from, and yet, indebted to its models.

Cast Iron

In the second half of the nineteenth century, cast iron was the material of choice for the construction of shops, department stores, and the scores of commercial buildings that were being built by merchants in many cities. Its strength allowed for large glazed openings, ideal for displaying goods and providing generous daylight for manufacturing. Cast iron was also non-combustible, of great importance in dense cities where fire was always a concern. According to Margot Gayle, "In 1849 James Bogardus created something uniquely American when he erected the first structure with

Right: Plate VIII from *Illustrations of Iron Architecture, made by The Architectural Iron Works of the City of New York*, Daniel D. Badger, E. G. Lind, Herbert Mitchell, 1865.

Right and below: Haughwout building, 488–492 Broadway, New York, John P. Gaynor, 1857.

self-supporting, multi storied exterior walls of iron. The innovation was its two street façades of self-supporting cast iron, consisting of multiples of only a few pieces. Merchants and wholesalers, the best customers for iron-front buildings, also responded to another advantage of cast iron architecture—the speed and economy with which it could be constructed. The many sections of an iron facade were cast at the foundry in molds, then finished and the smaller parts assembled and bolted together."[13] Because the material was molded, it could be used to reproduce the masonry elements of historic buildings, columns, arches, carvings that would have been too costly to provide in stone. Cast-iron facades reveled in the use of repetitive components, arrayed without variation, and architects and builders mined historical precedents for inspiration. As Gayle observed, "Especially favored was a window motif derived from the Roman Colosseum or from Sansovino's library in Venice. It was comprised of arch springing from small columns, flanked by larger columns supporting an entablature."[14] This reproduction of large historic motifs was accompanied by the imitation of stone textures. Fluting, rustications, elaborate stone tooling, and individual stone patterns were all reproduced to create the illusion of ornate stone buildings.

While familiar historic architectural elements were being imitated, their relentless, uninflected repetition across whole facades was wholly modern: no axiality, no hierarchy. An architect or a builder could look at a foundry's catalogue and choose parts to build a new building or to put a new facade on an older building. James Bogardus and Daniel Badger, for example, published such catalogues offering a great variety of components that could be used, and repeated, in almost limitless permutations.

This architecture was based on imitation, repetition, pre-fabrication, and the interchangeability of parts and on the rediscovery of the module. In classical architecture, the module that organized the design of a monumental building was the diameter of the column; all the parts of the building and their spacing were multiples of that basic unit. In the design of cast-iron facades, the module was a large building element that was deployed over the whole facade as the organizing matrix for the placement of the catalogue parts. The classical module had taken possession of the factory.

Speaking of James Bogardus, the architect Philip Johnson noted:

As an influence on my own design work, Bogardus looms larger, let us say, even that Louis Sullivan. Even Richardson, a greater architect, was

Right: Daniel Badger, sketch of the Cary Building.

Above: 254–260 Canal Street, New York, James Bogardus, 1856/1857. A good example of the repetitive use of prefabricated modular elements.

not such a direct ancestor of mine as James Bogardus. It is, fortunately, easy to say why. With the cast-iron facades, he acquainted Americans with modular rhythm, which is the basis of modern design. Imagine Mies without a module. Imagine Le Corbusier without the basic freedom of regular spaced windows. When the International Style arrived here in the 30s, we Americans were ready. The Crystal Palace was on our minds, of course, but what was new was modules of iron and steel applied as curtain walls, which came to us directly, indigenously if you will, from James Bogardus . . . In the Seagram Building, Mies covered the structural frame with an infill facade of bronze plates and decorative colonettes, but the total effect is still infill modules, no axiality, no frieze at the top, no differentiations or accents in the facades.[15]

The use of modular organization, which became the most important characteristic of modern architecture, had its source in the imitative architectural practice of cast-iron architecture.

Old Forms
New Materials

WE TEND TO think of architecture in neat, closed categories: archetypal forms tend to be well defined in our mind's eye. A house, a barn, a loft building, a basilica, those words evoke images of buildings built in certain, immutable ways, with certain materials. Similarly, modern archetypes have their rules. We expect them to be abstract and devoid of ornament and to use glass generously. In other words, we expect that there is a direct correlation between the archetypal form and its material expression. What happens when architects experiment with these limits and reclaim familiar archetypes for contemporary use? This chapter examines six projects whose designs use "remembered forms" with new esthetic and material expressions: The Dairy House, an addition to an existing building in Somerset, England; the Memu Experimental House, a new house prototype in Hokkaido, Japan; Trollbeads House, the extension of an existing office building in Copenhagen, Denmark; the Cantzheim Vineyard Guest House and Orangerie, the addition of two small buildings to an existing manor house in Kanzem an der Saar, in Germany; 16 West 21st Street, a new apartment building in New York City; and the Basilica di Rete Metallica, a partial re-creation of a ruined basilica in Siponto, Italy.

   In all cases, the starting point is a familiar form. Whether they are local vernacular building types or a more universal type, the new buildings act as metaphors for the remembered forms and the way in which the new

work engages the source image—how close to it or how far from it—
is what stimulates our interest. Through this transference, we
understand and experience a familiar form in a new way, and the new
building's role as metaphor in relation to the source image engages the
memories associated with it to form a continuous chain.

The word "metaphor" is used here in an attempt to characterize designs
that build on formal connections with known models, without necessarily
literally replicating them and by doing so harness the emotional and formal
power of these antecedents while at the same time extending their life.
This strategy depends on "likeness and analogy." Metaphor is defined by
the Merriam Webster dictionary as "a figure of speech in which a word
or phrase literally denoting one kind of object or idea is used in place of
another to suggest a likeness or analogy between them (as in drowning in
money) broadly."

Kenneth Frampton has noted that "Metaphor, rather than being solely
a linguistic or rhetorical trope, constitutes a human process by which we
understand and structure one domain of experience in terms of another of
a different kind."[1]

This strategy then becomes a critical social factor if one believes with
Gabriel Tarde that "A social group is a collection of beings as long as they
are in the process of imitating each other or as long as, without imitating

themselves in fact, they resemble each other and that their common characteristics are ancient copies of a same model." [2]

Because the question of the building form is often quickly settled by this imitative strategy, the architect's focus shifts to materials and construction. There is always a change in materials, and this material transfer from the old form to the new usually goes along with intensive material research. The new materials and their placement can introduce porosity and light in previously opaque envelopes and develop new craft practices for the realization of the remembered form—the introduction of layered glass in a timber wall in the Dairy House, the development of an articulated curtain wall in the Trollbeads House, the use of rammed earth for Cantzheim guest house, the substitution of glass for masonry in the West 21st Street building in Manhattan, or the substitution of wire walls for masonry in the Basilica. The act of building is also rethought in relation to the remembered form, and the new construction processes constitute a new form of craft. Their reference is not to "industry" but rather to making by hand; even when the building's components are high-tech (as in the Dairy House or the Trollbeads House), their assembly and design celebrates "making." In the Cantzheim guest house, the rammed earth makes the very act of making, and the time required for it, visible in the texture of the walls.

The Dairy House

Somerset, UK

2007

Skene Catling de la Peña

Above: The original dairy house, left, and the addition, seen from the garden.

Opposite: Evening view of the addition bridging between the original building and the hill.

This project involved the enlargement of a nineteenth-century masonry dairy house built by the owner's great grandfather for the estate's cheesemaker. The addition fills a narrow space dug into the hill behind the existing house providing additional bedrooms, bathrooms, and more generous circulation spaces. The building sits in an 850-acre estate in Somerset, and the addition was to be discreet, invisible from the main facade of the existing structure and "undesigned," a natural extension of the old building.

The architect refers to the project as a dogtrot[3], the vernacular American building type consisting of an open center passage—for the dog to trot— flanked by two enclosed living spaces. She also refers to it as a "folly." The addition can be read as a dogtrot in its recessed center, in plan, emphasized by the void of the pool and framed by two rooms; it is also, perhaps, a three-dimensional dogtrot since the ground floor is a void framed by the new building above and the ground because the addition bridges from the old house to the hill. The dogtrot/folly pairing suggests a fantasy of the simple life but also a fantasy of escape and freedom.

The addition has the archetypal form of a house, or a barn, and it looks like it could be older than the building to which it is added. At the start of the project, Charlotte Skene Catling was inspired by seeing timber planks drying nearby; the raw planks were separated by spacers for air circulation. This generated the idea and aesthetic of the extension.

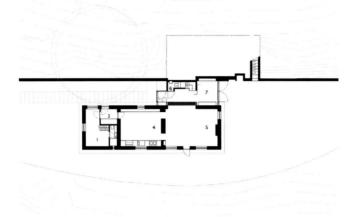

Ground floor plan

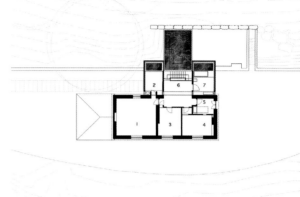

Second floor plan

Above: Exterior wall of the addition.

Opposite: Glass layers alternate with wood boards; on the right, glass layers are turned to allow views out.

Glass "boards" would be layered in the same manner in the new design, becoming thicker towards the base to reinforce a sense of weight and rustication. The new building envelope is porous to light; its form is old, but its concept and execution are new.

Textured, weathered wood boards, left rough on the outside but planed smooth on the inside, contrast with the rigorous precision of the glass, itself rough on the outside but polished on the inside. The apparent simplicity of the dairy—a primitive hut—and its position as a folly in the woods suggest an escape from the formality of the estate.

The glass receives the same level of care as the wood planks but is produced industrially by Pilkington, with a high degree of precision— a super technological product; it is installed with gaskets and caulking to resolve the different dimensional tolerances between glass and timber in a system developed through trial and error by the architect and a local craftsman. In three areas, the glass "boards" are turned vertically as narrow horizontal windows.

Glass is the interstitial material, but it is at the core of the project's conception; ideas of transparency and reflection associated with glass animate the project. There is the reflection of the two symmetrical rooms in the pool, there is also the laminated glass-and-timber wall reflected in the bathroom's mirrored wall giving the sense of an infinite forest.

Above: The addition at night, seen from the hill.

Opposite: The addition and existing building at night, seen from the garden. An opening in the retaining wall leads to the exterior stair to the pool above.

Below: Longitudinal section through the pool looking at the addition and the existing building behind it. The space for the exterior stair to the pool level is on the left.

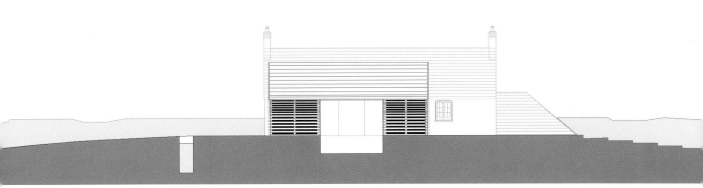

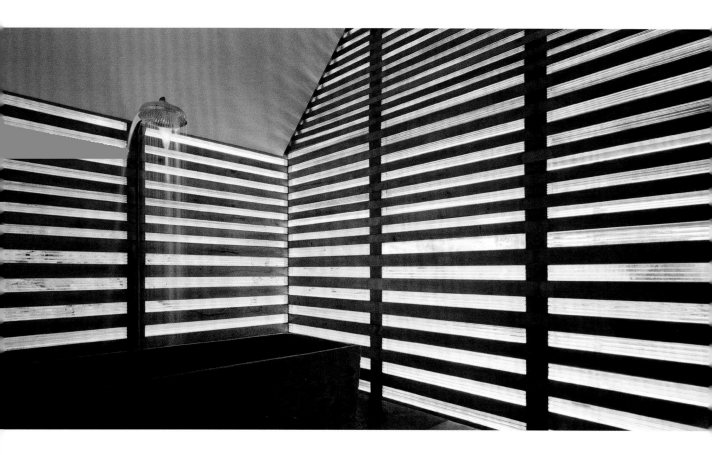

In the Dairy House, a modest, timeless vernacular form has been transformed into a highly refined combination of dark and light, old and new, antique and modern, rough and refined. What is the relationship of this design to memory? Obviously, the simple barn form speaks for itself and numerous other "un-designed" buildings, modest shelters, countless vernacular buildings. We know these buildings in our heart. They are realized in different cultures in different materials, but the simple roof form and the material, cultural, connection to "place" is always there. The introduction of highly crafted, highly engineered glass and the juxtaposition of this modern industrial product with traditional materials and construction transforms the traditional form into something else: a sensual, highly intellectualized, object, in the present. The architect uses palpable qualities of craft: specific individual boards harvested and dried in place; their texture and relationship to the glass display the act of making. It is all local, derived from tradition, and all manual. What appears un-designed is highly designed, what appears traditional uses re-invented traditional practices combined with modern industrial processes to achieve a traditional object of the mind or perhaps a fantasy of contextualism.

Opposite: Bathroom.

Opposite below: View into addition and existing building beyond from the pool.

Right: Passage between the existing building and the addition. The glass slot on the floor denotes the boundary between old and new.

Memu Meadows Experimental House

Hokkaido, Japan

2011

Kengo Kuma & Associates

The traditional house of the Ainu, the original occupants of the island of Hokkaido, was a simple, rectangular volume with a pitched roof, clad in layers of dried grass. Familiar because all the houses in the village were the same and all oriented east–west, the building was an archetype whose origins nobody knew. Such buildings have an uncontestable authority and a density of presence that cannot be created *de novo*; they are collective works and the work of time. But it may be possible to reproduce some of the qualities of this archetype into a living, transformed, new building.

This experimental house was designed by Kengo Kuma & Associates to test sustainable solutions to habitation in extreme climate. The Memu Meadows Center for Research of Environmental Technology is a "laboratory" assembling a collection of experimental houses built under the auspices of several universities and research institutions (Waseda University, 2011; Keio University, 2012; Harvard University, 2013; the University of California, Berkeley, 2014).

Kuma was inspired by the traditional house of the Ainu people, the "Chise" or "House of the Earth," which was built with local materials. As he has explained, "Bamboo leaves, wild grasses, thatch, reed grass, and tree bark were used for roofs and walls, which were tied with grapevine or tree bark. The wood of chestnut, Japanese Judas trees, and Amur maackia were used for supporting pillars; these were directly set up without

Above: Traditional Ainu house.

Opposite: Translucent polyester replaces thatch in the Experimental House.

foundation stones. A Chise has three windows: the one in the back is a rorun-puyar (god's window), through which the gods entered, the one on the right is for letting in the light, and the one near the entrance is for cooking ventilation . . . A "Chise" was 33 to 99 square meters in area. It was a warm and comfortable home of the Ainu in the old days." At the center was a fireplace whose fire was never allowed to burn out: "The fundamental idea of Chise, 'house of the earth' is to keep warming up the ground this way and retrieve the radiation heat generated from it."[4]

With the Experimental House, Kuma transferred the thick layering of grass and leaves into a thinner layering of modern artificial materials, produced industrially. The house is constructed with larch framing and clad with a layer of translucent polyester insulation, sandwiched between polyester fluorocarbon cladding on the exterior and a removable glass fiber fabric on the interior. The insulation was made from recycled PET (polyethylene terephthalate) bottles. "We do not treat insulation within the thickness of the heat-insulation material only, which was a typical attitude of the static environmental engineering of the twentieth century. What we aim at is a dynamic environmental engineering to replace it for this age. That we utilize the radiant heat from the floor is part of it ."[5]

As in the traditional house, there is a fire pit in the center of the open space, and the new house is sitting directly on the ground, Straw mats incorporate a system of heat piping. There is no artificial lighting, although

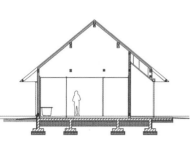

Cross section

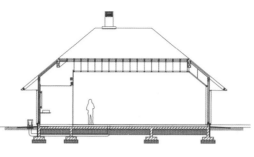

Longitudinal section

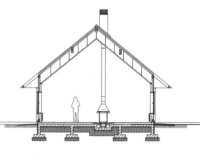

Cross section looking at hearth

Opposite: The translucency of thermal insulation admits natural light to the interior.

Opposite below: Interior of a "chise" in Ainu Village Museum in Shiraoi, Hokkaido, Japan.

fluorescent tubes at the base of the walls make the house glow at night. "Without relying on any lighting system, you simply get up when it gets light, and sleep after dark. We expect this membrane house enables you to lead a life that synchronizes the rhythm of the nature."

Opacity has been replaced by translucency, ordinariness and familiarity by uniqueness and experimentation; local natural materials installed by residents have been replaced by highly processed industrial products installed by professionals. Is this new house simply a replication of the traditional "Chise" of the Ainu built with different materials? Superficially, the only similarity between them is their size and shape. The new materials are very different visually, to the touch, and they probably smell and sound unlike the old dry grasses. Is it possible that this transference will give a new life to the archetype and allow it to be built again instead of surviving in folk museums? Maybe the most intriguing or evocative transfer is the core idea of the old house, the fire pit with a constant fire that warms the ground and its straw mats. If we agree with George Kubler that "copies continue a sequence unraveled by the prime object. But they also prove that formal sequences exceed the ability of any individual creation to exhaust its own possibilities,"[6] the prime object and this copy are part of the same sequence whose formal possibilities still exceed both the prime object and the copy. In this project, the "formal object" includes the deeply symbolic house form, its orientation, and the fire pit at

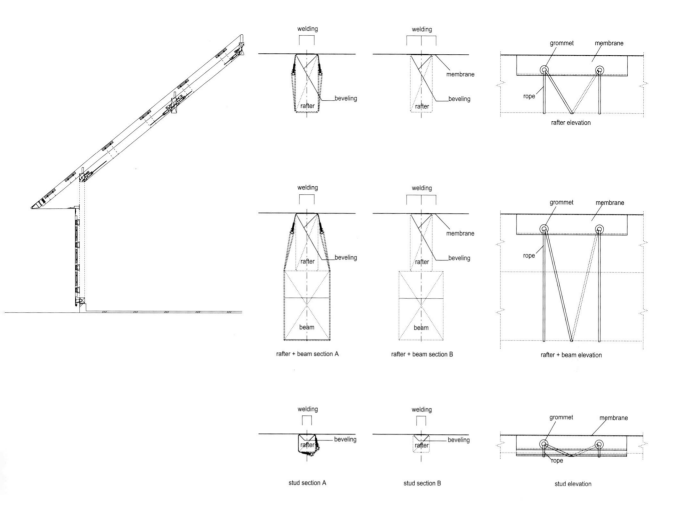

welding

beveling

rafter

welding

membrane

beveling

rafter

grommet membrane

rope

rafter elevation

welding

beveling

rafter

beam

rafter + beam section A

welding

membrane

beveling

rafter

beam

rafter + beam section B

grommet membrane

rope

rafter + beam elevation

welding

beveling

rafter

stud section A

welding

beveling

rafter

stud section B

grommet membrane

rope

stud elevation

Opposite: The translucency of the material and the windows admit natural light to the interior. Fluorescent tubes at the base of the wall add a glow inside and out.

Above: Membrane construction details: membrane section at eave; studs and rafter sections showing how to secure exterior membrane with rope threaded by hand through grommets, a contemporary craft practice.

its core, but also some less tangible elements like insulation and light. It is interesting that Kuma focused on the environmental characteristics of the "Chise" house: to keep warming up the ground and retrieve the heat generated from it. This concept, along with the decision to omit artificial lighting, points to a desire to recover some of the life qualities of the traditional house and to use contemporary materials within the environmental strategy of the old house. So the new house, through the old house, tries to re-establish an ideal state of balance, a kind of stasis within nature, in that particular place.

Trollbeads House

Copenhagen, Denmark

2013

BBP Arkitekter

Above: Street view before the intervention showing existing building recessed from the street line.

Opposite: The expanded building built out to the street line.

The curtain-wall design of this new building and its material are related thematically to the owner, a manufacturer of glass and gold beads. The building is, in fact, an expansion of an office building whose facade— a conventional 1960s curtain wall—was set back from the street. This facade and the roof were demolished and the existing floors extended to meet the property line at the street. The "new" building provides showrooms, storage, and manufacturing with a penthouse apartment for the owner at the top. BBP Arkitekter sees it as a Venetian merchant's house with raw material delivery at the bottom, showroom, fabrication on the floors above, and living quarters at the top.[7]

The goal was to design a building that would be integrated in the streetscape. The expanded building adopts the profile of its six-story neighbor and wraps this historic shape in an articulated curtain of hinged, horizontal strips of perforated copper stretching from the ground floor at the street, over the roof, and down over the rear facade. "Between the two curved party walls, a skin of glass is stretched to cover the roof and facades. On the outside a golden copper alloy 'curtain' is hung, making a kind of inverted curtain wall. Areas of the copper curtain can simply fold up to generate a pattern of fenestration matching that of the adjacent buildings and giving continuity to the streetscape. When closed the pattern becomes homogenous and impenetrable—but then dissolves to reveal the interior with lighting at night."[8] This curtain is clearly expressed as a

Above: The new building during the workday, in the evening, and at night.

Opposite: The articulated curtain wall closed over the windows for security.

separate layer, moveable in parts and applied over the armature of the transverse end walls, which are readable in profile and also in elevation as recessed reveals between the building and its neighbors.

BBP saw the problem as one of relationship between "the modern and the historic," noting that the challenge was "to make a modern building with the same construction principles as the underlying 1960s building that also fits in the street and the historical context". The answer was to conceive of a different kind of curtain wall—an articulated crafted curtain in front of a simple glass wall. The facade is punctuated by a series of windows whose size and placement are similar to those of the adjoining six-story building, but the window pattern continues over the roof, conveying the non-structural quality of the copper curtain: "It's like a textile, like a fabric on a chair, you put it on and then you wrap it softly down around the curve." The window pattern is not static. During the day, it can be visible, or not, depending on the time and the movement of the shutters in the curtain. At night, the modern glass building shows though the veil, and the window pattern disappears; the facade becomes porous as the interior light filters out through the finely perforated copper material.

The new curtain wall is highly crafted. The surface of the copper slats is finely perforated in a pattern, designed by textile designer Lene Toni

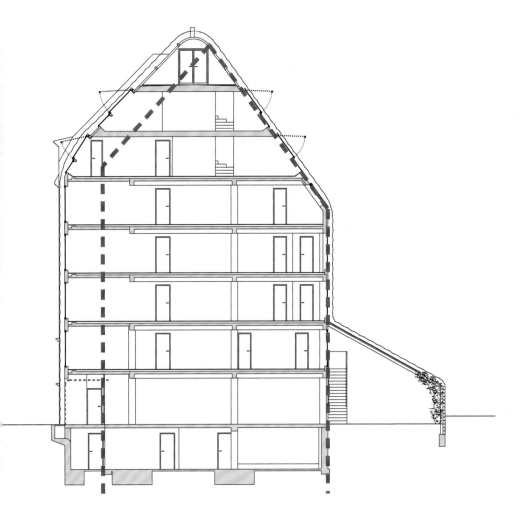

Above left: Building cross section showing relationship of the existing building section (red dashed line) to the new building profile.

Above right: Street view before intervention.

Opposite: Aerial view of the new building profile in relation to the traditional building forms.

Opposite below: Isometric diagrams showing the structural extension of the existing building; the closing of the new shape with windows and spandrels; and the sheathing of this enclosure with the articulated metal curtain.

Kjeld and intended to evoke a "hedge of thorns guarding a treasure." The slats are hinged to create the window pattern; where the curtain wall does not move, each panel is stretched like a fabric over and under horizontal metal rods to affirm each slat dimension. The new curtain wall "is a play with the volume instead of roof, facade, windows," and it is conceptually consistent with the logic of the curtain wall of the original building.

A comparison between the 1960s facade and the new facade is instructive: the earlier curtain wall proclaims its machine-made, mass-produced, prefabricated lineage—spandrels, windows, muntins, and window frames are all familiar catalogue items.

In the new building, the prefabricated facade assumes a secondary role behind the crafted copper curtain wall.

The copper curtain wall appears highly crafted in the way it is assembled and in its metaphorical allusions. Elements have been designed and fabricated specifically for this building; their texture and joinery speak of

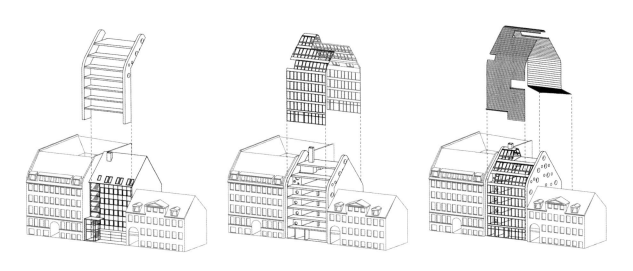

Above: Copper curtain over windows
in open position

Opposite: Copper curtain

Opposite below: Drawing of the "hedge of
thorns" pattern in the copper slats

how they came to look this way and work this way. The perforated pattern
was machine made, but its reference to a "hedge of thorns" and its
fabric feel deny any industrial reference. Similarly, the delicate assembly
of the copper slats has a finely articulated texture associated with pre-
industrial products. "The hinge becomes an ornament. It has a function, but
it also becomes part of the ornament . . . I try to get something out of
the way it is made to have more of the traditional way—to have a feast out
of the way it is made."

This new building integrates a number of seemingly contradictory
elements: traditional punched windows pierce a thin curtain of copper
and then disappear in this curtain at night; a highly crafted, highly
tactile moveable curtain floats in front of a generic glass facade and
then becomes the roof and its entire skin; the material, a golden copper
alloy, which has oxidized to gray, is machine made, but its color, texture,
and joinery are all meant to evoke craftsmanship. In the end, a new
understanding of craft and manufacturing is put in the service of place.

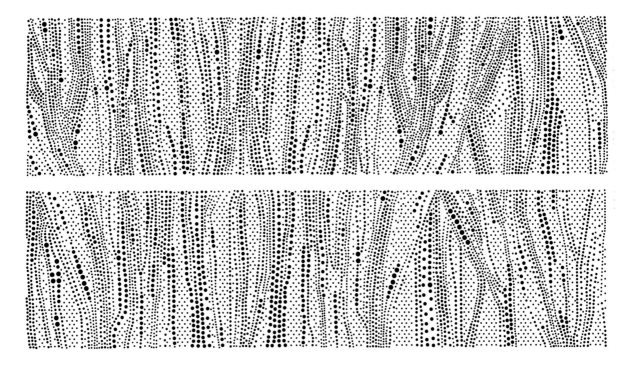

Cantzheim Vineyard Orangerie and Guest House

Kanzem an der Saar, Germany

2016

Max Dudler

Above: View of the Cantzheim buildings from vineyards on the hill. The guest house is on the left, the manor house in the center, and the orangerie on the right.

Opposite: Guest house.

Built in 1740, the manor house of this winery was originally used by the Premonstratensian monks and later by the Episcopal Seminary of Trier. Vineyards provide a physical and emotional backdrop for the buildings: row upon regular row ascend the steep hillside, a potent representation of an enduring way of life.

Acquired by private owners in 2007, the historic building has been restored. Two new structures have been added on the long axis, but the disposition is not symmetrical: one building's ridge is aligned with that of the manor house and the other is at right angle to it. Both have a simple house form, with a low-pitched gable roof, but the form and materials are different. The remise, which is used as a guest house, is a two-story structure with rammed-concrete walls and roof; the orangerie which is used for meetings, is built of a series of identical metal frames with glass infill panels. The remise is dense, monolithic, and opaque and the orangerie is light, articulated, and transparent; the historic manor house is the centerpiece of this non-symmetrical symmetrical arrangement.

The rammed-concrete building has an unquestionable presence, commanding attention for its density and diagrammatic quality, but its pairing with the orangerie makes for a fine essay on the myth of the simple house form, on the infinite ways it may be built and crafted and still retain its power, embedded in a place, and yet universal. With the remise, the house form is a volume reduced to its most basic elements—walls, door,

Above: The manor house mediates between the transparency of the orangerie and the solidity of the guest house.

Right: Site plan

Below: Longitudinal elevation with orangerie to the left and guest house to the right

Opposite: The landscaping of the courtyard complements the geometry of the guest house.

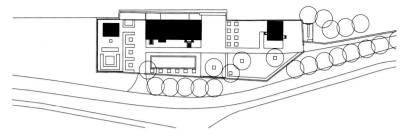

untrimmed window openings, and a chimney—and two materials—rammed concrete and oxidized bronze. The surface is all important: its unity is crucial for the realization of the icon, but its crafted quality and its texture of irregular layers make it tactile so that the abstraction comes to life with palpable materiality.

The owners chose rammed concrete to integrate the new building in its setting. According to project architect Simone Boldrin,

> The choice of material came from the place, suggested by antique constructions present in the vineyards which form the Palatinate's hilly landscape. We are talking of small monolithic stone buildings, which seem to take their form and be born from the soil, called, for their similarity with the buildings in Italy's Puglia, "trulli". Built and still used as shelter and as tool storage by the vineyard workers, they insert and camouflage themselves perfectly in the landscape because of their size, materiality and because of their archaic form. Just like these constructions, the *remise*, as a service building in the new winery, had to be born from the stone of the earth and to become part of the setting of the vineyards that are the backdrop of the late baroque manor house, so as to reinforce the *genius loci*.[9]

The rammed concrete, which uses sand from the Rhine, anchors the new building in the place and also makes it a part of the vernacular masonry tradition. The material inserts the new building in a tradition of masonry craft: walls made by hand, layer by layer, a process visible in the texture of the walls. The owners like to point to a specific layer they rammed themselves and is imperfect. They saw an added value in this material because of the way it was built, by hand, by craftsmen and artisans who were "first person" authors of the work, in spite of the risk involved in a material whose possibilities and limitations were not fully known. As Stephan Reimann, one of the owners, observed, "It's alive; when it rains it gets darker and when it dries, it changes again, and you can see all the layers because of the different densities."[10]

On the other side of the manor house, the orangerie does some of the same things visually, but in a different way. It too is a simple house form with a minimum number of elements: repetitive metal frames resting on a low rammed-concrete wall, a glass surface, and double doors at opposite ends of the space. Here the house form becomes transparent and sheds its references as a shelter.

Opposite: Steps on both sides of the guest house provide access to the interior.

Above: A traditional agricultural storage building in the region.

Right: The progress of construction of the guest house can be read in the rammed-concrete wall.

Above and opposite: Orangerie.

The orangerie is light, its relationship with the landscape is one of transparency and its material relationship to the land is tenuous:

The monolithic part of the orangerie is reduced to a swelling from the earth, it is born from it. The building's footprint on the ground delineates an empty volume, as if it were the negative of the *remise*. In the case of the *remise* the material takes up the whole space and forms every detail.

Could it be that this variation on the house form allows the new buildings to be both familiar and new, "hot" and "cold", referent and

abstract? The relationship of the remise to the *locus*, through the local specificity of the material, its kinship with the "antique" forms of the small vineyard shelters and dry masonry walls, and the visible representation of the labor of the people who made it, is extremely compelling. On the other hand, the orangerie provides a cool counterpoint to rebalance the whole composition. This strategy seems to invent a contextual relationship with the historic manor where a connection with the past is forged through a familiar form but then abstraction and a material transfer transposes it to our present.

16 West 21st Street

New York

2009

Morris Adjmi Architects

Above: Upper floors of 16 West 21st Street in context.

Opposite: 16 West 21st Street flanked by early twentieth-century masonry loft buildings.

The facade of this narrow, fourteen-story residential building in the Ladies' Mile Historic District is an idealized rendition of the design of the turn-of-the-twentieth-century commercial buildings of New York and particularly those in this historic district. Its organization of base, large middle section, and attic floor articulated with broad spandrels can be seen in the neighboring buildings and all through this area around the Flatiron Building.

Here the monochrome facade is made of slumped, pressed, and carved glass, which gives the building an unexpected translucent quality— an interesting sensory overlay over the traditional loft masonry facade. In certain light conditions, when sunlight hits the facade in the morning for example, a glow seems to emanate from the building so that a form associated with opaque masonry becomes penetrable and light. Rather than an exchange of opacity for transparency, this is more a case of the exchange of a certain kind of opacity for a different kind of non-transparency. The glass has a physical presence and varied textures, some evoking brick patterns through a pattern of lines imprinted on its surface.

The familiarity of the building form allows Adjmi to experiment with the relationship of material to form in a neighborhood where "jarring" new architectural expressions are frowned upon by the Landmarks Preservation Commission, which is responsible for approving new designs in the area. By now, glass has become synonymous with "modernity;" in its use in twentieth-century commercial architecture, the defining aspects of this

material are transparency, abstraction, and absence of ornamentation.
The audacity here is twofold: a historic form is remembered—a distillation
of multiple memories of this building type—and then built in the most
unlikely material. Here glass is neither a modern material (no transparency,
abstraction, absence of ornamentation) nor a historic material (no
precedent for its application or its particular form of textural ornamentation).

In approving the design as "appropriate," the Landmarks Preservation
Commission found that "the overall development of the tripartite facade into
base, shaft, and crown reflects a typical pattern of facades in the Ladies'

Mile Historic District; that the proposed glass facade will be a contemporary evocation of the taller historic buildings in this historic district, and molded glass will recall the features which are found on historic buildings of a similar scale."[11] Appropriateness here is understood as keeping historic patterns of composition relevant through new procedures, which does not preclude a non-historic use of materials to achieve a "contemporary evocation."

The choice of color was critical. In fact, white was the generator of the design; the building is located in the Ladies Mile Historic District, mostly built after the White City of the World's Columbian Exposition in Chicago of 1893 transformed American cities. This district is made up of "white" masonry buildings built of buff brick, terra-cotta, and stone. For Adjmi "the building had to be white," but not the white terra-cotta or buff-colored brick of older buildings but a "modern" material reproducing the old form but at the same time adding to its possibilities.

The composition of the facade and its scale and disposition of elements are familiar, but it is an abstraction representing the idea of a New York loft building. The choice of glass to build this distilled historic form makes the

building both generic and unique: it is connected to its very specific place while also transcending it to claim a certain building type.

Morris Adjmi refers to Roland Barthes and his reflections on photography in *Camera Lucida*: for Adjmi "it is all in the balance between the *Studium* and the *Punctum*:"[12]

> It is *studium*,... application to a thing, taste for someone, a kind of general, enthusiastic commitment, of course, but without special acuity. It is by *studium* that I am interested in so many photographs, whether I receive them as political testimony or enjoy them as good historical scenes... The second element will break (or punctuate) the *stadium*... it is this element which rises above the scene, shoots out of it like an arrow, and pierces me . . . This second element which will disturb the *studium* I shall therefore call *punctum*; for *punctum* is also: sting, speck, cut, little hole.[13]

The *studium* of the "good historical scene" of the White City is in balance with the *punctum*, the "sting" of a new material expression for the old form.

Basilica di Rete Metallica di Siponto

Puglia, Italy

2016

Edoardo Tresoldi

Above: Aerial view of the site showing the existing basilica of Santa Maria Maggiore, the first basilica partially reconstructed in metal mesh, and the open archaeological excavations.

Opposite: The partially re-created basilica, looking toward the apse.

The early Christian basilica of Santa Maria Maggiore in Siponto, near Manfredonia, was destroyed by an earthquake in the eleventh century; only its foundations and a few mosaics remain. Standing next to the ruins is the current basilica of Santa Maria Maggiore completed around 1117: parts of this Romanesque building, columns, capitals, and decorations were probably built with spoils from the older building. The town of Siponto was abandoned after the earthquake of 1233, and this site is now an archaeological park.

This publicly funded project was initiated in an effort to renew interest in the site. The early Christian basilica's presence, its volume, and its placement are evoked by a diagrammatic construction built of welded galvanized-steel wire mesh *(rete metallica)*, produced by Cavatorta. Edoardo Tresoldi describes his approach to the project: "The path began with a research of historical records with experts, archaeologists, and professionals of cultural heritage. When this topic came into my world, I began to imagine a sort of return of this great building, as if it were part of the historical memory of the place."[14]

The first basilica is reconstructed in part, "drawn in the air," in the words of the designer. Its incompleteness alludes to a state of ruin, but its fresh, new, consistent materiality feels like a construction drawing where every element is described and explained by its presence but also by its interruption. The sequence of arches along the nave is interrupted in the

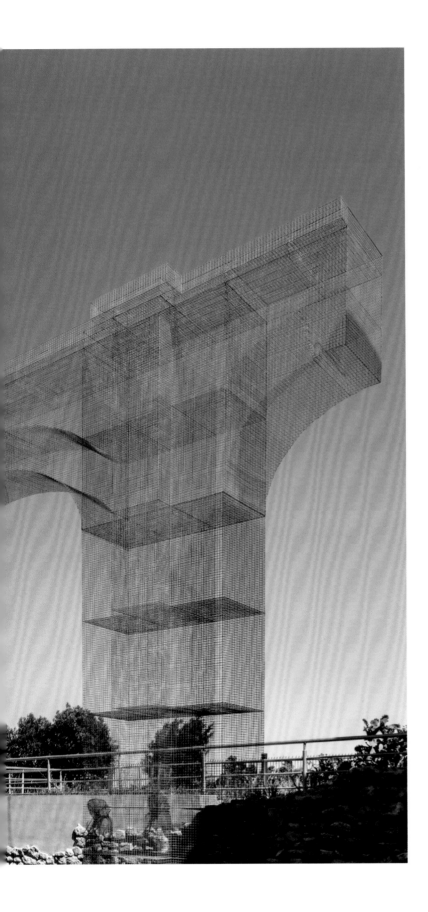

Opposite Partially recreated basilica with
Santa Maria Maggiore in the background.

Below: The nave and apse.

middle, the rafters are cut in mid-length, and more importantly the wires in no way pretend to be a replication of the original masonry. It is clear that this is an entirely new building. Forms such as vaults and arches, born out of the requirements of load-bearing masonry, are recreated in a thin transparent veil of steel mesh. Architectural elements are shown in a diagrammatic way; columns, column capitals, arches, vaults, roof framing can all be seen at the same time because of the transparent quality of the wire mesh. They seem present but somehow abstracted.

This is a building intended to evoke an earlier building "over time." It is as though the construction process—and perhaps, symmetrically, the destruction process as well—is made visible by the building's transparency and its incompleteness. Tresoldi has titled the project "where art re-constructs time," and he talks about "absent matter." This new/old building triggers questions about then and about now and all the moments in between.

The building assumes a completely different presence at night where the transparency of the wire mesh surfaces plays less of a role against the dark sky. The surfaces and volumes become denser, and one becomes

78**78** MATERIAL TRANSFERS

Opposite: Apse during the day and at night

Below: Columns and arches showing metal mesh surface and the horizontal webs used as reinforcement.

much more aware of the interior spaces and the generating lines of their geometry because of the inner "framing" of the wire walls. Neither view evokes use or human interaction with the new structure except from viewing and contemplation—relevant uses in themselves, however.

What does this change in the material reality of the original building produce? What does it add to our understanding and our experience of this site? Or of other sites that contain building ruins visible only from the air and difficult to experience? Obviously, this is a contemporary art project with a strong conceptual basis; it is an idea. It evokes but does not reproduce; it suggests an image that is slightly out of focus; it privileges volume and architecture over surface texture and decoration and the general perception of the architecture over the incidents of surfaces. It makes the building a-historical. It invites the viewer to imagine—because so much imagination is required—but also, perhaps, to reflect on the constancy and relevance of certain archetypal forms, which transcend their time-bound material realization.

New Forms
Old Materials

THE RELATIONSHIP OF vernacular architecture to "high modern" architecture is fundamental, but it is often forgotten.

In the usual practice, an architect draws inspiration from a particular vernacular form or a particular vernacular building type and brings those forms into the domain of contemporary architecture, generally through a process of abstraction and material changes. Thus, Le Corbusier's "journey to the east" in 1911, through Austria, the Balkans, Greece, and Turkey, provided him with a vocabulary of building forms, materials, and building practices that he never forgot and that are central to understanding his architecture.

In the four projects discussed in this chapter, the process is reversed as architects start with non-archetypal, modern, abstract forms and combine them with traditional materials: a half-timber screen, gabions, or thatch are used to create unexpected hybrids; the Garden Building is a new residence building at Saint Hilda's College, in Oxford, UK; Dominus Winery is also a new building in Yountville, California; the retreat center for the Brothers of Tillburg is an addition to an existing group of buildings in Vught, The Netherlands; the Wadden Sea Center is a visitor center for a UNESCO World Heritage Site in Ribe, Denmark.

The combination of assumed universality inherent in the underlying modern forms of these buildings and the specificity of material, craft, and place is what makes these projects compelling. They go beyond the easy simplification of "modern" versus "traditional" materials and make a claim for a broader view of architecture based on multiple continuities—the continuity and relevance of contemporary architectural expressions, the continuity of local material usage, and the continuity of local craft cultures. Local materials and traditional techniques are transferred from the traditional forms with which they are associated to modern forms. This involves experimentation with builders and crafts people in order to adapt traditional techniques to new building forms. Modern forms, abstract, ideal, seemingly independent of the here and now and un-sensuous (touch, smell) are brought down to earth by the use of a traditional, often formless, materials with intense textural and experiential materiality.

This results in a new condition where the drive to abstraction, to the universal, and to industrial processes inherent in the modern aesthetic, is tempered with a deep interest in the specific, the local, and the crafted building.

Garden Building, College of Saint Hilda's

Oxford University

Oxford, UK

1970

Alison and Peter Smithson

Above: Little Moreton Hall, Cheshire, acknowledged by Peter and Alison Smithson as an inspiration.

Opposite: A corner showing the structural supports for the timber screen and its relationship to the concrete-and-glass building behind it.

In the summer of 1967 the College of Saint Hilda's approached the architects Alison and Peter Smithson to design a building that would offer "a maximum number of study-bedrooms together with some Fellows' Rooms."[1]

The Smithsons designed a four-story square block with chamfered corners in plan and a shallow service court at the back. The facade has two layers. The inner layer consists of large plate-glass ribbon windows over low concrete spandrels stretching horizontally across the facade: a modern building in glass, concrete, ribbon windows, all organized in a repetitive pattern. The outer layer is a timber frame applied in front of the modern facade, expressed as a truss of horizontal and diagonal oak beams resting on the triangular brackets projecting from the sides of precast-concrete columns.

In Robin Middleton's article "The Pursuit of Ordinariness," a set of small illustrations documents the architects' "Inspirations." First on the list is a sketch by Louis Kahn of a concrete structure with the connections between vertical posts and horizontal beams emphasized, captioned "detail from Louis Kahn's famous sketch suggesting that architecture resides in the joints"; two other illustrations show traditional half-timber buildings in England and in Germany, where horizontal, vertical and diagonal timbers form the structure and the facade, and indeed the whole building. There is also a photograph of a timber bridge at Magdalen Boys School, Oxford.

Left: The building sits in a mature landscape.

Right: Konrad Wirtz, *The Annunciation*, c. 1440. A reproduction of this painting was included in the Smithsons' scrapbook and acknowledged as an inspiration.

The next illustration is a detail of a painting by Konrad Witz; the detail, supposedly from a postcard in the Smithsons' scrapbook, focuses on the wood column and its diagonal braces to the two beams above. This source is particularly suggestive because, in the painting, the wood column and its articulation are separate and in front of the wall, a relationship similar to the one between the oak "lattice" and the wall at Saint Hilda's. Middleton comments that "the oaken lattice at St. Hilda's, whatever functional purpose it might serve, is conceived as a *jeu d'esprit*; a playful adjunct, harking back to the architecture of the past, to the lattice screens of Tunisia, to the black beams of sixteenth-century England and to a more localized garden bridge."[2]

The overlay of a vernacular idiom on a high modern, Brutalist building softens the diagrammatic quality of the building and turns it into an ambiguous, friendly but recessive, presence deeply rooted in its place. Instead of being a simple manifesto, it becomes intriguing and moving because of the risks the architects took in such a gesture for which there was no structural basis and no accepted intellectual justification at the time. The Smithsons wrote that this exterior oak screen was designed to provide visual privacy to the young women, but it is difficult to believe that it fulfills that role in any other than a symbolic manner. It is more likely, as Middleton suggests, that the Smithsons wanted "to evolve an acceptable and useful vernacular."[3]

This project is particularly relevant because of the date of its construction, 1970. The mature period of postwar modern architecture was over, dominated as it had been by the abstract glass forms of American corporate modernism. In the late 1960s and early 1970s architects started reconsidering the relationship of their work to the existing world and worked to find ways to reintegrate the forms and materials of old buildings into their thinking and into their way of work. With this in mind, the Smithsons' identification of their sources is particularly important, and in fact, revolutionary since "true" modern architects were not supposed to look to the past for inspiration. Here they name vernacular sources (half-timber, generally because illustrations show an example in Germany and an example in England, a local bridge, the timber bridge at Magdalen Boys School) and an art source (Konrad Wirth) as inspiration for their work; the sources are named and clearly credited with inspiring the work: the new building is now part of a historical continuum (the half-timber) and rooted in its place (the local bridge). In hindsight, the architects' explicit methodology and this particular design open the door to many of the projects in this book.

Opposite: The Garden Building in the campus context.

Right and below: Oak screen and concrete support brackets.

Dominus Winery

Yountville, Napa Valley, California

1997

Herzog & de Meuron

Above: The gabion wire cage (open at the top and with an additional wire screen below) with its stone infill and the twisted wire ties.

Opposite: The building set in the vineyard.

An abstract, precise modern form is built of imprecise rocks held in wire cages, an old alpine technique used to build earth retaining walls and military defenses. This ideal form sits in the middle of vineyards, commanding in its abstraction and yet absorbed in the color of the soil. "You could describe our use of gabions as a sort of stone wickerwork with varying degrees of transparency, more like skin than traditional masonry," note the architects.[4]

Wine making is intensely local; the same grapes will not produce the same wine in a different area. At the core of the culture, the craft and the art of winemaking is the concept of terroir, a word that comes from the French *terre*—earth, soil, land. A terroir embodies the land, the soil, the climate (sometimes the most closely observed micro-climate), the vines, and the human culture that occupies and is affected by the land. The terroir is the soul of the wine, and the wine is the embodiment of the terroir.

In Yountville, the Dominus winery is located on 120 acres of the former Inglenook estate called Napanook, whose grapes were responsible for some of California's best cabernets. The Napanook vineyard has a unique terroir, with a gentle 5 percent slope up to the Mayacamas Mountains that Christian Moueix, the owner of Dominus, regards as perfect for cabernet sauvignon.[5]

Describing the program, the architects explain, "The building is divided into three functional units: the tank room with huge chrome tanks for the

first stage of fermentation, the Barrique cellar where the wine matures in
oak vats for two years, and the storeroom where the wine is bottled,
packed in wooden cases, and stored until it is sold. We designed to house
these three functional units in a linear building some 100 meters long,
25 meters wide, and 9 meters high. The building bridges the main axis, the
main path of the winery, and is thus in the midst of the vineyards. Vines
in California can grow to a height well over two meters, such that
the building is completely integrated into the linear, geometric texture of
the vineyard."[6]

The choice of the gabion technique had the advantage of providing
natural climate control for the interior of the building: the stones form an
inert mass that insulates the rooms from the heat during the day and from

the cold at night. The local basalt rocks range from dark green to black and blend naturally with the surrounding land from which they come. The building, as abstract as it is, seems at times to become one with the earth.

Its abstract, ideal shape is anything but generic, and the exterior wall is crafted like wickerwork, almost woven. There is a variation in the texture of the wire cages as the density of rocks and the type of mesh vary to allow for different kinds of light penetration into the inside. The building is of the land and it breathes naturally. Its geometric shape alludes to a universal ideal, but it is specific and local. The new object, specific and ideal, modern and ancient, adds to and enriches the formal sequence born in the culture of modernism: it does not turn its back on this origin but builds on it by going beyond its limits.

Retreat Center for the Brothers of Tilburg

Vught, Netherlands
2001
Marx and Steketee Architects

This project, on an estate at the edge of Vught, a medium-size city in the Netherlands, consists of the threading of several wings into an existing series of buildings built and expanded over the course of three centuries.[7]

Marx and Steketee was selected through a competition organized by ZIN, a new entity formed by the Brothers of Tilburg, a lay order, and Bicker, an organization seeking to invest in educational ventures geared to mid-career business people. The existing structures included a two-story building in the center (originally an eighteenth-century hunting lodge with a second story added in the nineteenth century), flanked on the right by a chapel and, on the left, by another two-story building; behind the chapel was a utilitarian barn, itself an addition and practically in ruins.

The intervention consists of the addition of an auditorium building to the right and a new residential wing at the rear as well as the reclaiming and expansion of the barn. A narrow, two-story link connects the auditorium wing with the existing buildings; this new "spine" is, at times, absorbed into the buildings and, at times, visible from the outside. The scheme is direct, pragmatic, and logical.

The key formal idea is the displacement of the boundary between the old and the new. The auditorium is clearly modern, a horizontal volume with a flat roof whose solid upper story floats on a glass base. This upper section is clad in thatch, a traditional material whose soft edges, scupper details, and weathering are powerful reminders of the material's vernacular

Opposite: Auditorium at night.

origins. This is a hybrid form alluding to the co-existence of two time periods, two aesthetics contained in the same building. The clear boundary between the auditorium [new] and the existing building [old] is shifted by the choice of materials to the boundary between the glass base [new] and the solid volume of thatch above [old], itself under a flat roof [new]. The barn continues this theme: a clearly modern wing projects under a new roof, which is a simple extension of the old roof, with no apparent joint or modification. The spine connecting buildings follows the same rules. In plan it is a consistent element that links all the parts of the project. In three dimensions it takes on several guises. It principally appears as a two-story link between the new auditorium and the old building, but on the rear, it becomes a new facade for the existing building; indoors, the design is inflected as it moves through the buildings.

But it is the thatch that is a manifesto: its "formlessness," the unexpected use of an ancient vernacular material in a contemporary institutional project and its integration in a modern building form, all create a sense of surprise.

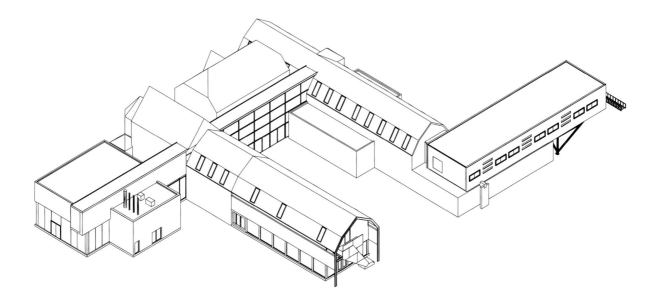

Opposite: Overall view of the complex with the new building on the right.

Above: Isometric drawing of the complex.

Below: Evening view of the auditorium showing the thatched upper surface and the lower area of glass.

The use of thatch to execute an abstract modern form is also significant because, over time, its surface appearance changes as it weathers over time. When newly installed, the material has a bright straw color which over time changes to a dull grey. In time the surfaces will have to be re-thatched. This represents a profound challenge to modern architecture's ideal of aesthetic permanence. Time becomes part of the design; the building restates our relationship to the past by deliberately eliminating the boundaries between "modern" and "traditional" materials and by using traditional materials to construct contemporary forms. In so doing, the building also eliminates the boundaries between "high" and "low." But perhaps the most important aspect of this new sensibility is the new freedom with which the architect is now able to take a building "as is" and work with it as neither an undervalued object nor an untouchable relic.

Wadden Sea Center

Ribe, Denmark

2017

Dortre Mandrup

"I believe that a building can enhance a landscape—increase the drama or underpin its beauty when placed correctly and when shaped aptly, " Dortre Mandrup asserts.[8] Located at the edge of the vast marshlands, which are home to millions of birds and other creatures, the Wadden Sea Center embodies the architect's beliefs about place and form; it is also engages the relationship between modernity and traditional crafts and materials, in this case thatch.

The Wadden Sea was listed as a UNESCO World Heritage site in 2009, recognized as "the largest unbroken system of intertidal sand and mud flats in the world . . . It is a large, temperate, relatively flat coastal wetland environment, formed by intricate interactions between physical and biological factors that have given rise to a multitude of transitional habitats with tidal channels, sandy shoals, sea-grass meadows, mussel beds, sandbars, mudflats, salt marshes, estuaries, beaches and dunes . . . Wadden Sea is one of the last remaining large-scale, intertidal ecosystems where natural processes continue to function largely undisturbed."[9]

This building is one of three designed by Dortre Mandrup at the edge of the Wadden Sea; this project adds a new building to a group of existing older buildings to form a new complex. Mandrup explains that the building "is an interpretation of the local building tradition and the rural farmhouse typology significant in the area. The center is erected with thatched roofs and facades, hereby underlining the tactile qualities

Opposite: Approach to the building.

Opposite: Walkway under thatched eave.

Top: Courtyard between the new building with thatch walls and roof and the existing building re-sheathed in wood.

Above: A glass wall, with views into the exhibition space, marks the entrance.

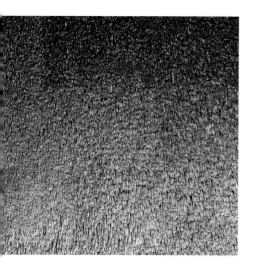

Right and below: The contemporary thatch enveloping the Wadden Sea Center contrasts with the traditional roof of a house nearby.

and robustness that can be found in traditional crafts and materials of the region."[10]

The modern form is striking in its horizontality; it is both in repose and dynamic, the shape seems almost molded but it is also very sharp. And this unique, modern form is built of a traditional material, thatch. However, in its local traditional use, thatch is used for roofing only. Here, to emphasize the building's form, the walls and the roof are made of thatch only, which except for modern glass windows and doors, is the only material of the new building's envelope. The non-traditional form challenged the thatchers to rethink the entire logic behind their traditional techniques. The large eaves on the north side, with their striking sharp edges and deep overhangs required new solutions within the techniques

of the craft. "These sections required a special combination of reeds and a reinforced underlay that could both secure the reeds and allow them to move over time." [11]

In a 2019 exhibition about her work at the Danish Architectural Center in Copenhagen, Mandrup stated that she is "interested in shapes" and that "working with thatched roofing does not spring from rediscovering an old craft; it's because it has a wonderful materiality." In her "unsentimental dialogue with tradition," using this craft allows the design to function well as a contemporary form, as a contemporary form in that particular landscape, as a contemporary form in that particular culture, but the intense materiality of the new building also gives new relevance to an old craft.

Mimesis
In Defense of
Imitation

"Remake, re-use, re-assemble, re-combine, that's the way to go."[1]

The eight projects in this chapter all unabashedly play with imitation, duplication, reproduction. Material and formal shifts are then layered on this basic conceptual strategy. The writer and architectural theorist Quatremère de Quincy has observed, "In truth, the pleasure that is produced by works of imitation proceeds from the act of comparing. It is certain that the eye and the mind, whose operation is here the same, are required to judge, and in order to judge, they must compare, deriving enjoyment only from this twofold condition."[2]

Indeed, for each of them, the inspiration for the new building is obvious, whether the old building is on the same or an adjacent site or the source is so well known that it will be obvious to everyone seeing the new work. The architect then devotes a great deal of thought to the material and craft realization of the new building in relation to the materiality of the original structure. Our pleasure, both sensual and intellectual, comes from comparing the old with the new and seeing their commonalities and their differences.

These projects demonstrate great diversity in materiality, and they all utilize mimetic strategies in the development of their design. The Hotel and Youth Hostel in Paris reconstructs a double building destroyed by fire. FRAC, Halle AP2 in Dunkirk, France, extends an adjacent building by replicating it. The Glass Farm in Schijndel, The Netherlands, replicates an idealized version of a historic building type, at a larger scale; similarly, Crystal Houses in Amsterdam replicates an adjacent building at a larger scale. 53 Great Suffolk Street in London uses the form of an existing building on-site as a model, while the design for 85 rue Championnet, a new apartment building in Paris, reproduces the appearance of the neighboring building and the form of the new visitor center for the Musée de Cluny, also in Paris, is indebted to that of the Gallo-Roman ruins on the site.

This mimetic procedure turns the original building, or the context, into an essential point of reference; it becomes literally indispensable, a step in a continuum that cannot be ignored. The new work would lose a great deal of its meaning if the source building were to disappear. The new and the old are inextricably linked, which makes this an interesting preservation strategy.

In these projects, the mimetic strategy is the key to the material transfer. Generally, through experimentation the architect develops new materials, or new applications for existing materials, in order to relate and, at times, to contrast with the duplicated form. The architect works with manufacturers in the laboratory but also in the builder's workshop, in a collaborative trial and error process, at times contributing digital files to the CNC machines.

In some projects, the mimetic strategy is almost a manifesto—a provocation, a challenge to accepted procedures. The architects redefine the relationship of new to existing. What emerges is a duplicated form executed in different materials with a different conception of the relationship of structure to expression, or with a different conception of the relationship of materials and representation (as in the building at 85 rue Championnet, in Paris). Does the authoritative, familiar form of the source image, somehow, help to usher in the new, familiar and yet different? Or has the very presence of the source building, visible nearby, freed the architects to experiment with the limits of reproduction and duplication?

Could duplication become a new legitimate tool in the arsenal of the modern architect, **an** invitation to reconsider the definition of the new and to expand it?

Hotel and Youth Hostel

Paris, France

2008

Chaix & Morel et Associés

The Magasins Généraux of the La Villette docks were built in the mid-nineteenth century to provide storage for grain and flour at the edge of Paris. The double warehouses were situated on either side of the Ourcq Canal, on axis with the Barrière de la Villette by C. N. Ledoux at the center of the opposite side of the long basin. In the late 1980s, after the decline of milling and warehousing in the area, the buildings were used by artists and artisans as workshop, office, performance, and exhibition spaces.

After one of the warehouses burned to the ground in 1990, a competition was organized for the design of a new building, and the firm Chaix & Morel received the commission. According to the architects:

> This new building, which houses a hotel, a restaurant, and a youth hostel, is welcoming and open onto the city. An obvious relationship of kinship is established with the existing warehouse of the Magasins Généraux ("general stores"). The airy cut-out evocation of the old massing forms a light silhouette that stands in contrast to the 1850 building. The interior courtyard lets sunlight into the heart of the block while creating areas of user-friendly circulation that benefit from exceptional views of La Villette Basin.

> The new building's formal outline—its double gable end, its size, and its placement—duplicates the original warehouse's outlines, and this evokes the urban and architectural setting before the fire. This is the "kinship"

Opposite: New and existing building facades facing the La Villette Basin.

Opposite and above: Views from the La
Villette Basin and from the bridge over the
Canal de l'Ourcq

Left: Aerial view.

Opposite: Atrium in the new building.

Above: View from the bridge over the Canal de l'Ourcq to the Rotonde de La Villette showing the relationship of the old and new buildings within the urban context.

the architects mention. The surviving building is a massive, symmetrical composition, built of rough rubble stone with sharply dressed stone at the corners, top of base, around windows, and at what would be the entablature of a temple fronted building. Its twin "stands in contrast," its volume enveloped in a lightweight lattice, porous to light and views. The buildings share the outlines of their volumes and their position across the canal, facing the dock, but otherwise they are quite different.

This addresses the need to re-establish the original symmetry and placement—the importance of urban preservation is satisfied by the mimetic volume. At the same time the desire to engage contemporary architectural expression is satisfied by the construction and materials of the new building. Mass is replaced by surface, opacity is replaced by porosity, stability is replaced by movement. The old form is executed in a radically different construction system with light materials seeming to float horizontally across its surface. The combination of mimesis and invention allows the new building to serve two masters: permanence and change.

FRAC (Fonds régionaux d'art contemporain)

Halle AP2

Dunkirk, France

2015

Lacaton & Vassal

Above: East elevation.

Opposite: The opaque, hierarchical facade of the existing building is juxtaposed with the translucent, non-hierarchical cladding of the new structure.

The project called for the adaptive reuse of a 1949 warehouse to house public collections of contemporary art for display on site and to manage the conservation, lending, and storage of the work. Lacaton & Vassal describe their concept:

> The North region FRAC is located on the site of Dunkirk port in an old boat warehouse called Halle AP2. Halle AP2 is a singular and symbolic object. Its internal volume is immense, bright, impressive. Its potential for uses is exceptional. To implant the FRAC as a catalyst for the new area and also to keep the halle in its entirety becomes the basic idea of our project. To achieve this concept, the project creates a double of the halle, of the same dimension, attached to the existing building, on the side which faces the sea, and which contains the program of the FRAC. The new building juxtaposes delicately without competing nor fading. The duplication is the attentive response to the identity of the halle.

Duplication of the existing form with new materials is intended to juxtapose without competing or disappearing. The form of the original warehouse is the carrier of emotions and cultural continuity, the carrier of memory.

The new building is a double building: the existing warehouse, a cast-in-place concrete volume with gable ends, a simple sloped roof, and

Above: Exhibition hall in the existing building.

Right: Cross section showing the different spatial treatment of the open "Halle" and the levels inserted in the new building.

Opposite: Space between existing building and new building, seen from top-floor bridge between the two.

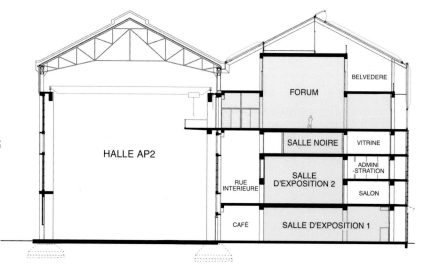

HALLE AP2

FORUM

BELVEDERE

SALLE NOIRE

VITRINE

RUE INTERIEURE

SALLE D'EXPOSITION 2

ADMINI -STRATION

SALON

CAFÉ

SALLE D'EXPOSITION 1

Opposite: The Forum, at the top of the new building, is used for events and exhibitions.

Right: The stair in new building abuts the translucent exterior wall.

a gridded facade expressing the concrete structure of the wall and the new building, made of light-weight "bioclimactic" material, a light, translucent skin of corrugated polycarbonate on a steel structure that is barely expressed as a non-inflected grid. The two buildings—a single entity—react to light in different ways. The warehouse is dense and opaque except in the centered symmetrical figure of glazing in the gable ends; the addition is light and translucent, its skin generating light at night and emanating a soft glow during the day.

Duplication turns the original building into an essential point of reference. While it is the unquestionable source for the new project, it is not frozen in the past because it is made to interact with the new building as a foil, as an anchor, and as "another place," somewhere to go to that is different, yet the same.

Of course, this puts into question the accepted belief in the necessary relationship between function, construction, materials and form. If the form of the original warehouse was the direct result of its program (a large storage facility), and of its reinforced concrete structure, then the new building, which presents the same form in a diaphanous plastic skin, has reduced—or is it distilled?—the essence of the warehouse to its size and to its shape. Does this enhance or devalue the older building? But then again, the original building was never—just—the logical, inescapable result of its construction system and its program. Were the shape of the roof and the design of the gable ends absolutely necessary with this construction system or were they, too, a transfer of an older form—a temple form, a barn form, a house form, both remembered through a new technology?

The Granary

Barking, London, UK

2011

Pollard, Thomas, Edwards
Architects

Above: The site before the intervention; the narrow brick building and the large gabled building are incorporated in the new project as is the small square building between the two.

Opposite: West facade of the complex with the rear of the new building on the right.

The Granary is situated along the Roding River in Barking, a former industrial district that is being developed as a residential quarter. Although some older buildings are being saved, the area's industrial character is disappearing so the preservation of this listed warehouse, built in 1870, and the support of its form and character are a particularly important aspect of the project. The unoccupied building had become derelict as the industries that sustained the area's economy left; a 2009 master plan called for a new Creative Industries Quarter centered on the Granary and the nearby Malthouse buildings.

The project consists of the adaptive reuse of the warehouse as offices and the addition of a new headquarters for the contractor/developer firm that bought the building. This was one of the first projects to be completed in the area, and its surroundings have changed dramatically as apartment buildings have been built close to it.

The design uses a very light touch with the older building and a bold, somewhat mimetic form for the addition, executed in bronze cladding, chosen in part for its tone and color compatibility with the warehouse. Foreground and background, boldness and deference are engaged in a continuous dance in all aspects of the project. "The new is both a dramatic statement and a delicate intervention," as Teresa Borsuk of Pollard Thomas Edwards observes.[3]

The new building is clearly separate from the warehouse; it is juxtaposed

Above and opposite: Street and aerial views.

to it a few feet away: "The new extension is attached to the original building via a vertical circulation core and a high-level bridge link" so that the two buildings are related and may function as one but remain distinct.

The addition relates to the old building in several ways. First, the altered mimetic form of the end wall, which we perceive as a gabled wall, is clearly a nod to the warehouse roof line, but the new roof line is not symmetrical, indicating that something else is at play. As one walks around the building, the simple end wall becomes part of a dynamic prismatic form, visually autonomous but still linked to the warehouse building. "if you look at the building head on, it is a pedimented building, but if you look at it in three dimensions or if you look at it sideways, you then realize that it is a trapezoidal building. It is a mass as opposed to a facade and a roof. This other has a facade and the roof sits between the gable ends. But in form terms this new building is different," Borsuk explains.

The design and placement of the windows in the addition provide another visual link with the warehouse. The windows, at the gable end of the addition act as a kind of displaced replication of the warehouse windows: they are punched opening, but cut out of a bronze skin rather than thick masonry; they are aligned with the warehouse windows, but not as symmetrically ordered, and they are spread, as windows on all the surfaces of the new prismatic form, walls and roof. While the asymmetrical gable form is a visual link to the masonry warehouse, the window treatment

Opposite and above: The entrance to the complex through a passage between the buildings. A bridge connects the two at the upper level.

Above right: Massing models testing forms and color relationship between the old and the new

emphasizes the envelope of the new building as a skin, a wrapper, whose surfaces are treated equally. "There is a strong connection between those windows and what is existing, that's what holds it all together—we spent a long time looking at these openings because in historic buildings, everything seems very ordered, but there is also some disorder," Borsuk concludes.

The choice of metal cladding—a bronze alloy named TECU made by KME Engineering—reflects the architects' intention that there should be respect but also sharp contrast in the relationship of the old and the new. The cladding had to be a skin since it needed to cover the walls and also the roof, and while this uniform envelope is very different from the wall/roof relationship in the warehouse, its color and tone are compatible with the warehouse. Here again we have an element that may be read both as assertive and connective.

The altered mimesis of the new facade is the key gesture that grounds the new building in its particular place and in its particular relationship with the existing building; it also evokes all the similar forms embedded in our cultural memory, where the form of the warehouse also resides. This immediate grounding and the complex links to an existing building culture allow the architect to move the new building form and its expression into the "now." The design is generated from the place, and it also participates in the global contemporary architectural culture.

Glass Farm

Schijndel

Netherlands

2013

MVRDV

Above: The market square after the buildings along Hoofdstraat were demolished in the 1950s and before the construction of the Glass Farm.

This all-glass building stands at the edge of the market square in the village of Schijndel in North Brabant in the Netherlands. As in other areas of the Netherlands, many buildings in Schijndel were destroyed during World War II, but those lining the main street were demolished in the 1950s when the city council decided to create the market square. Historically Schijndel was a linear town, and the weekly market was held along the main street. The new square was not successful; the space was too large, and it lacked activities to attract people.

In the 1980s, the architect Winy Maas, who had grown up in the town, started campaigning to replace the lost structures with a new building. Over more than thirty years, the project took on many forms for different programs, including a new theater, and it was the subject of intense debate among the residents. but eventually an agreement was reached to build shops and community spaces, and this was to be a "farmhouse," which "then became a symbol of the town's growth over time. Its proportions not only ensured that the design could avoid giving the impression of misplaced nostalgia, but also emblematized the fact that while Schijndel literally had outgrown its farming roots, it certainly did not deny them."[4] The maximum built envelope permitted by the local planning regulations approximated the form, but not the size, of the region's traditional farmhouses, and the idea to use this form for the new building took root. According to the architect, "All of the remaining farms of this type were

Above: The Glass Farm at dusk looking
toward the market square

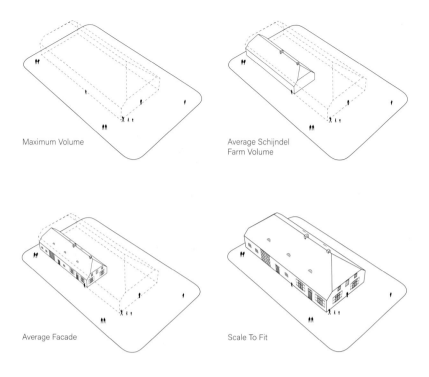

Maximum Volume

Average Schijndel
Farm Volume

Average Facade

Scale To Fit

measured, analyzed, and an 'ideal' average was developed from the data. In collaboration with MVRDV, artist Frank van der Salm photographed the historic buildings, and from these a collage of the 'typical farm' was composed. This image was printed using fritting procedures onto the 1,800-square-meter glass facade, creating an effect similar to stained glass windows in a cathedral."[5]

The Glass Farm is scaled 1.6 times larger to create a monument to the traditional building.[6] The new building provides the desired edge to the open space of the market square, and it is at the same time assertive and elusive: assertive in its imagery but also elusive because the relationship of the new building to the "model" presents a puzzle. On parts of the roof, the printed image is at times invisible because the glass reflects the sky; the pattern of bricks and windows is visible on some walls, but the reflection of adjacent buildings can negate the perception of solid materials. On other walls the "farmhouse" is more readable, but perceptions change with each building surface and viewing perspective. We associate the image of a farmhouse with a specific set of sensory experiences; we expect a certain relationship between what we see (a brick wall for example) and what we can touch. While some of this information is visually given by the photographs, it is denied by the single material—glass—and

Above: Lorem ipsum ade sunt, totasit hil
et es re audae numquun tiaeri.

Above:: View from Hoofdstraat toward
Saint Servatius Church on the square.

Below: Longitudinal section showing
retail uses on the ground floor and office
and community uses above.

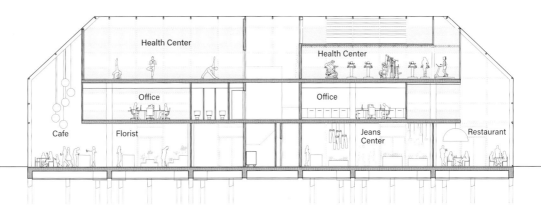

its reflective quality. Doors and other elements such as vents are part of the photographed, idealized, farm walls, and the architect makes sure that the viewer understands that the building is a representation of something else and not the thing represented itself. See for example the odd bubbled openings in the brick pattern to allow views from inside. This transfer of scale and imagery uses the power of memory, and illusion, in the service of an urban gesture; it honors the source image while at the same time making us intensely aware of its inaccessibility.

When one steps inside through the "brick" doors, the impression is a different one. The glass wall is no longer reflective, and the images have a great immediacy. We forget the expectations prompted by the exterior image; the overall familiar form of the farm has been replaced by a series of color "slides" of enlarged building elements which are familiar but have

Opposite and above: Scaled-up features of local traditional barns, brick wall, windows and shutters, terra-cotta tile, and thatch roof are printed on the glass surface of the facade.

become separated from an overall building form, and we are in a kind of upside-down space. We are looking at the back—or is it the front— of the walls and the roof, and we see magnified textures and unexpected incidents—a leaf on the roof tiles, caught on camera and there forever. At times it looks like we are looking at an old building very close by, across the street, and at times it feels like we are looking "through" the brick wall. Everything has been enlarged, and we can enjoy looking at the building textures and colors which become more real than real. Rough, smooth, coarse, glossy, or matte surfaces and saturated colors surround us, but divorced from their relationship to the archetypal building form, they become decorative. Pictures of the roofing materials (thatch, terra-cotta tiles) are on the ceiling and pictures of the walls, with their brick construction and punched windows, are on the walls of the new space, but otherwise the new steel structure supporting this envelope follows its own logic, independent of its relationship to the printed images. But it is the richness of the colors, the immediacy of the photographed textures, and the appeal of what they represent that make the experience of the interior intensely satisfying. At night, the cinematic quality of the building evident inside becomes even more intense.

This building is, somehow, elusive: the idea of reproducing an old building in a modern medium is in the air, whether it is a photograph or a laser-cut image. It satisfies our desire for historical and contextual continuity and also our belief in the value of "the new." The Glass Farm is an experiment with how real, or not, to make the illusion, and how to create a satisfying new building at the juncture between illusion and reality.

Opposite: Customers at a café table juxtaposed with over-scaled bricks and window.

Above right: Brick wall and tile and thatch roof.

Right: Restaurant at the ground floor.

Crystal Houses

Amsterdam, Netherlands

2016 for Chanel

2019 for Hermès

MVRD, Gietermans & Van Dijk

Above: Glass bricks between the glass frames of the shop windows.

Opposite: The facade incorporates glass bricks and glass window frames on the two lower floors, with a transition to traditional bricks at the top of the second floor and a brick wall and traditional windows above.

Glass bricks are not a new thing. The development of "Walls of Light" in the early part of the twentieth century is an important part of the history of modern architecture, connected as it is to new developments in lighting technologies and the construction of a certain image of modernity. The glass blocks of the late 1920s and 1930s were used, in their most iconic manifestations, in the development of modern forms intended to depart from historical precedents.

Crystal Houses represents the opposite of that approach: here glass bricks are used to build a quasi-duplicate of the historical form of two buildings that once stood on the site. The project replaces two three-story buildings that were part of a three-building row (the third remains on the right, a witness of the original design and size of the two demolished buildings), with two buildings in "the same design," but vertically stretched, literally, to provide a larger retail volume. The taller ground-floor masonry wall was built anew with solid glass bricks; in the middle of the second floor, the glass wall gradually morphs into the traditional brick; at the third floor, the exterior wall is entirely brick. The genesis of the idea is clearly in the physical and historical context of the site itself. As Winy Maas of MVRDV explains, "Crystal Houses make space for a remarkable flagship store, respect the structure of the surroundings and bring a poetic innovation in glass construction. It enables global brands to combine the overwhelming desire of transparency with a *couleur locale*

Below: The new building in context on Peter Cornelisz Hoofstraat.

Opposite: Transition from glass to brick at the top of the second-floor windows.

and modernity with heritage. It can thus be applied everywhere in our historic centers.[7]

The building form is modeled on the original, but it has been stretched vertically and its companionable relationship with its neighbor has been severed. Does it matter? It would be easy to answer this question by saying that this design is a corruption of a historical model, but while the material substitution is obvious, the stretching of the facade is harder to discern. A strict preservation theorist would disapprove as the new buildings give a false impression of historic reality and they have disturbed an ensemble of three buildings. But is there a counter argument that this new iteration as placed in the ongoing sequence of this particular building form, adds to it, and keeps it relevant through its material addition?

Looking and comparing brings the neighboring building into play—it is the indispensable protagonist. The careful observer will notice the flattening out of the facade at the upper floor of the new building, visible in the almost

flush condition of the window with the face of the brick wall, presumably the result of the fact that the new building is a steel-frame construction rather than load-bearing masonry.

The visual effect of the glass brick is particularly impressive from the inside looking out: the masonry wall texture and its transparency offer a new experience: the "old" brick wall is now a reticulated mass of glass bricks and high performance "mortar" (one does have to put the memory terms in quotation marks, because this is a very different "mortar" from the original, technically and culturally and in the way it is applied) which provides a wholly new version of the original wall. The scale of the bricks is identical, but the solidity of the old material is dissolved by the transparent glass. In the new Hermès store, the transition area of the facade where the glass bricks are combined with the terra-cotta bricks is now visible from the interior and one is able to see "the dissolving effect where the glass bricks meet terra-cotta bricks close up."[8]

This mimetic strategy is combined with an intense, cutting-edge research in material development involving specialized manufacturers in Italy, the Netherlands, and Germany and the Delft University of Technology. This is an entirely new building, constructed with unique materials developed in the laboratory rather than traditional crafted materials. Solid glass bricks were individually cast in Italy and put in place with a high-strength, UV bonded transparent adhesive. The construction site has become a laboratory and a material dating back to pre-historic building technology has been replaced by a cutting-edge "replica" developed by an international team of scientists and craftspeople. A historic form, the carrier of memories and the embodiment of "character," stability, unquestioned emotions is replicated with new materials proclaiming their modernity: the replica preserves our perceived link to the past and the laboratory based construction techniques appropriate the historic form and materials for the present—the technical tour de force is essential to this material and cultural transfer.

Previous spread, above, and opposite: The transition from glass to brick seen from the interior.

53 Great Suffolk Street

London, UK

2018

Hawkins Brown Architects

Above and opposite: Existing and new buildings on Great Suffolk Street

The original three-story building was built in the 1890s. The new building, constructed on the site of an adjacent garage, more than doubles the existing floor area to 40,000 square feet. Hawkins Brown's goal was "to create a new building that can be read as one whole, striking the right balance between being sympathetic to the existing warehouse and its special qualities but also to create a strong contemporary and contextual building."[9]

The duplicative strategy of the main facade design enhances the street presence of the original building by taking on its language and its form and restating them with some variations. A new cantilevered center stair serves both buildings and a floor added to the older building is cantilevered from the foundations of the addition, so the buildings are more functionally and structurally integrated than it would seem from the facade. Similarly, the language of the new building has invaded the original warehouse facade through the redesign of the center windows; all window openings, whether new or old, have been fitted with the same windows, forming an underlying framework holding the buildings together—the weft of both fabrics.

The form of the addition repeats that of the original building, and the design of the street facade follows the same rules of hierarchy and bilateral symmetry; within this general order, it introduces a very open ground floor entry, with a steel beam to frame it, in contrast to the arched openings in the original building's brick wall. This gesture is important as it makes it

Top: Site before construction with the garage building the addition replaced.

Above and opposite: Joint between the new and old.

Below: Side elevation of existing building before construction.

Right: Side elevation after the top-floor addition and the installation of new windows.

Opposite: New building entrance and decorative tile panels below the windows.

evident that the architect does not want to replicate the structural qualities of the old building. Once the decision had been made to replicate the form of the adjacent warehouse, the facade material need not have been brick and the choice of brick is indicative of the architect's acceptance of the scheme's transgression. Counterintuitively, it is the design's mimetic strategy itself that constitutes the strong contemporary statement, an ideological departure from an orthodox modern ethos forbidding imitation. Then it becomes possible, even desirable, to use brick: the new brick color and texture were chosen to distinguish them from those in the warehouse and to add variety to the texture of the wall. The bricks are then laid randomly throughout the facade, emphasizing the act of building and the "hands of the artisan."[10]

85 Rue Championnet

Paris, France

2017

Chartier Corbasson Architectes

Opposite: The apartment building is clad in a thin layer of TRESPA on which the image of the facade of the adjacent limestone building is reproduced.

Overleaf: The new facade with the shutters open and closed.

Since the middle of the nineteenth century, apartment buildings in Paris have followed rules established by Baron Haussmann, adhering to a maximum building envelope (*gabarit* in French). Whether grand or modest, buildings follow the same general pattern: they are built at the street property line, generally constructed of limestone, and topped by a roof with dormers. There is more or less ornamentation, there are more or less elaborate balconies at the piano nobile and at the upper floor, and the ceiling heights might vary with the building "class," but the pattern is the same. This manner of building was established between 1853 and 1870, but "Haussmanian" buildings continued to be built into the twentieth century closely following the original pattern but with stylistic accommodations to adapt them to current architectural and social sensibilities. Architects like Michel Roux Spitz (1888–1957) designed abstracted version of the older buildings, stressing horizontal lines and large horizontal windows in tune with the new modern sensibility, while still adhering to the traditional materials palette and building volume. The uniformity of the *gabarit*, continuity of horizontal lines, material tonalities, and basic design framework all contribute to the consistent appearance of Parisian streets and to their specific urban character.

In 2017 architects Karine Chartier and Thomas Corbasson took a different approach for a new building at 85 Rue Championnet, in a working-class neighborhood of Paris. While the earlier modern strategy had called on

Need High res

abstraction to interpret and update the historical model, here the architects call on replication to regenerate it. Innovation is found, paradoxically, in a copy.

The street facade is a thin layer of TRESPA, a wood resin material used for road signs, which incorporates the pixelated photograph of the building next door. The photograph captures the stone construction and its ornament (panels, cornices, modillions) as well as the metal railings. It also captures the facade at a particular moment: some windows are open, others are closed; some metal shutters are closed, most are open. The image is, in fact, not printed. Chartier and Corbasson were attracted to the material because its core is dark beneath a light gray surface. This made it possible to reproduce the image by machining the panel rather than printing on it. The panel is drilled through to create some transparency and

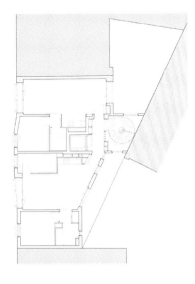

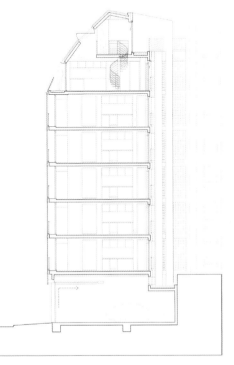

at the same time, in a larger circular "drill," the outer gray layer is etched to
reveal the darker material core and to create the pixelated image.[11]

In contrast to the permanence and solidity of a traditional Haussmannian
building, this skin is variable and mobile because it is mostly composed
of operable shutters that fold out, revealing, behind the skin, a modern
apartment building with floor-to-ceiling windows and glass balcony railings.
At once respectful and provoking the facade nods to its historic neighbor
as it plays with the very metaphor that is the basis of its design. The
image of a stone bearing-wall is paper thin, it bulges in the middle, opens
and closes at will. In the public realm of the street, it adopts the traditional decorum, but behind its protective layer is a thoroughly contemporary
apartment building.

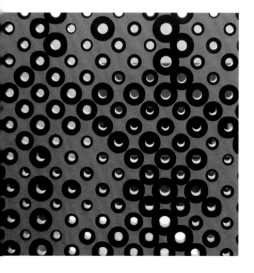

This image of a specific moment is animated as shutters open and close: the continuity of the new building with its historic model has shifted in intriguing ways. The overlay is not limited to the layering between the outer layer (image of the historical facade) and the inner layer (the "real" modern building). The outer territory itself is claimed by the modern building as the operable shutters do not correspond either in size or placement to the images of the windows. Chartier and Corbasson have fully embraced the possibilities of this strategy: "For us it is a question of integration and of establishing continuities with what exists . . . it is a question of working on materials, on mimetism for continuity."

The new building depends on its old neighbor for the pleasure we take in seeing their similarities and their differences. The different treatment of windows, the shockingly different construction of the same building image, the differences in materials and textures, and the differences in construction—all contribute to the experience. We take pleasure in the sophisticated, loving ironies present in the new work, but at the same time we take comfort in the continued relevance of the model.

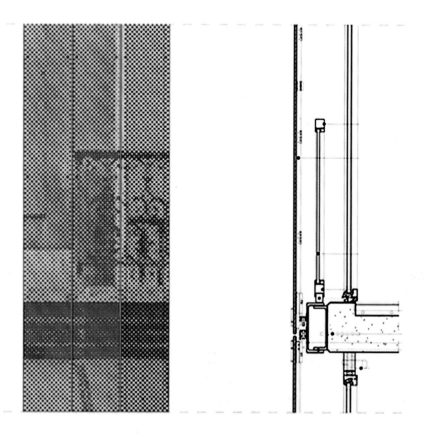

Above: Detail of a Trespa panel showing areas where the panel is drilled through and others where the surface is also eroded to expose the black core of the material.

Right: Panel reproducing a balcony railing.

Far right: Section detailing the relationship of the façade panels, the glass railing, and the window.

Opposite: A Juliet balcony with the panels open.

Visitor Center for the Musée de Cluny

Paris, France

2018

Bernard Desmoulin Architecte

Above: Reliquary of Saints Lucien, Maxien, and Julien, 1261–62, from the Sainte Chapelle.

Opposite: The visitor center from the Boulevard Saint-Michel.

The new visitor center for the Musée de Cluny provides "the site with an additional glow with the least impact on the existing structure." This statement from Bernard Desmoulin is a remarkable summary of the contradictions inherent in the program: how to bring visibility to a group of buildings with "the least impact"? How to be visible and invisible at the same time? Facing west on the Boulevard Saint-Michel, the simple double-gable roof profile of the new building continues the rhythm of the historic Gallo-Roman thermal baths immediately north of it, and, at times, its walls have the golden glow of a giant reliquary, an homage to one of the medieval reliquaries in the museum's collection. The new building takes its cues from the place itself, whether visible or hidden.

This historic site is a collection of buildings constructed at different times. The two dominant buildings are the Hotel de Cluny, a late fifteenth-century townhouse built as a residence for the abbots of Cluny (and restored in the nineteenth century) and the ruins of early third century Gallo-Roman thermal baths. The two buildings were not perceived as part of the same institution—The Cluny National Museum of the Middle Ages— and the baths seemed isolated and forgotten. The location and appearance of both buildings set them apart: the monumental baths, facing west on the Boulevard Saint-Michel, are built of rough alternating courses of brick and stone while the urbane Hotel de Cluny, overlooking Paul Painlevé

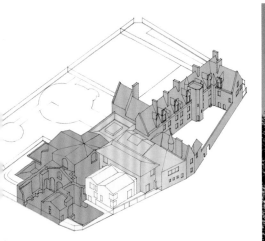

- = Thermal baths, 1st–3rd century
- = Hotel de Cluny, 15th century
- = 19th century updates
- = New visitor center

Right: The visitor center in the context of the archaeological excavations and the Gallo-Roman baths and house.

Above and opposite: On the entrance facade on the Rue du Sommerard, the varied textures of the aluminum panels respond to the patterns in the stone of the Gallo-Roman buildings.

Square, is built in finely dressed limestone. Desmoulin wanted to create a dialogue between these disparate elements—old and new.

The new visitor center gives the museum a new presence on the Boulevard Saint-Michel, a favorite destination for tourists; thus the newest building is juxtaposed with the oldest and brings it into the present while also bringing the Hotel de Cluny into play. The geometry of the baths' roof line is the generator for the form of the visitor center. The secondary facade, on the Rue du Sommerard, is more abstract, taking its place

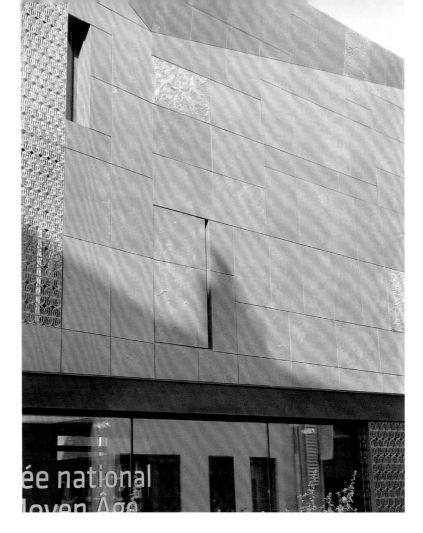

in a group of three buildings including the Hotel de Cluny and a nineteenth-century addition (with early twentieth-century alterations) built to imitate the wall construction of the thermal baths: here the visitor center has a recessive cubic form but still alludes to the baths' roof line with a shallow inverted gable form at the top of the wall, created by a subtle in-folding of the wall plane.

Exterior walls are made of cast aluminum panels of varied textures. The workers threw sand at the bottom of the molds before the panels were cast to create a random texture; no two panels are alike, and each carries the evidence, the memory of the moment of its making, and the memory of its maker. The reference is not to an industrial process but to labor, to making and individuality. The architect did not control the gesture, but he specified the number of panels to be produced in each texture and the way they are distributed on each facade. Desmoulin observes: "There is an element of workmanship, and that is what interested me. It is like the imperfections of the ruins—time has made it happen. It does not have

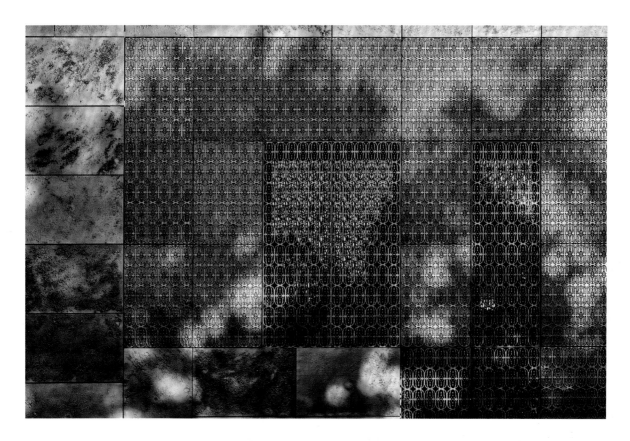

Above, below, and opposite: Textured
aluminum panels and open-work screens
on the visitor center refer to the materials
of the Gallo-Roman building both inside
and out. Various method were used to
create texture, including throwing sand at
the panel mold.

a definite design, and what interested me was the element of chance, imperfection, and the fact that it is the hand that has produced the texture, and also the fact that it would be different at different times of day. When light falls on the surface, it is caught in different ways depending on the relief."[12] Each facade also has a number of panels perforated in a pattern inspired by the stone enclosure of a circular stair in the Hotel Cluny; this treatment, used in front of glazed openings, allows the skin of the facade to remain taut, except for one large rectangular bay window.

The relationship of the visitor center to the existing buildings is based on two key ideas: one relies on composition and the replication of the outline of the thermal baths and the design of a more neutral facade to relate to the Hotel de Cluny. Mimesis plays a strong role in this integration of the old and the new and in the creation of an indelible, repeated, image. The other, equally important, idea is Desmoulin's desire to express time, and making, in design, as these two notions relate to the presence of the ruins on the site—their imperfection and their incompleteness—so that they may engage our reflection on the role of "chance, imperfection" and making in architecture.

Notes

Introduction

1. George Kubler, *The Shape of Time: Remarks on the History of Things* (Yale University Press, 1962), 71.

2. William Harlan Hale, "Art vs. Yale University: Challenging Yale's Girder-Gothic and Its Builders," *The Harkness Hoot* (11/15/30): 19.

3. Kubler, quoted in MVRDV, *Copy Paste, T2f (the why factory)* (nai010, 2017), 41.

4. MVRDV, *Copy Paste*, 42.

5. Louis Kahn, "I Love Beginnings," in Alessandra Latour (ed) *Louis I. Kahn: Writings, Lectures, Interviews* (Rizzoli International Publications, 1991), 288.

6. "The article considers the implications for Modernist architecture, poised on the knife-edge between the nineteenth-century tradition of copying (Boime) and the modernist strategy of originality (Shiff), and for the practice of architectural history." Abstract of Jan Kenneth Birksted, "The Politics of Copying: Le Corbusier Immaculate Conceptions," *Oxford Art Journal*, (6/1/07) 30 (2): 305-26, accessed 7/30/17.

7. CNC: Computer Numerical Control machines. Lathes, routers, and similar equipment machining metal, wood, or other materials and controlled digitally.

8. MOMA/Learning: Pop Art on moma.org.

9. Gabriel Tarde, *Les Lois de l'Imitation* (Les Empêcheurs de Penser en Rond, 2001), 128 (author's translation).

10. Rosalind E. Krauss, *The Originality of the Avant-Garde and Other Modernist Myths* (MIT Press, 1985), 170.

11. Paul Duro, *Why Imitation, and Why Global*? (Association of Art Historians, 2014), 625-26.

12. Kubler, 71.

Remembered Forms
New Materials

1. Kenneth Frampton, *Studies in Tectonic Culture: The Poetics of Construction in Nineteenth and Twentieth Century Architecture* (MIT Press, 1995), 6.

2. Philip Johnson, foreword to Margot Gayle and Carol Gayle, *Cast Iron in America: The Significance of James Bogardus* (W.W. Norton & Co., 1998).

3. Kubler, 71.

4. The attribution to Alberti has been contested. To the extent that the argument in this essay does not depend on authorship, I will not address this question here.

5. Rudolph Wittkower, *Architectural Principles in the Age of Humanism*, (W.W. Norton & Co, 1971), 41-47.

6. Wittkower, 47.

7. There is a precedent in the corner pilasters of the Baptistery of San Giovanni in Florence.

8. Wittkower, 42.

9. Julio Carlo Argan in *Paestum and the Doric Revival 1750–1830* (National Academy of Design, 1986), 12

10. Robert Wood and James Dawkins, *The Ruins of Balbek, otherwise Heliopois in Coelosyria*, 1757, and *The Ruins of Palmyra, otherwise Tedmor in the Desert*, 1753.

11. Dora Wiebenson, "From Palladianism to Greek Revival Architecture in America," in *Paestum and the Doric Revival*, 180.

12. Wiebenson, 180.

13. Margot Gayle and Edmund V. Gillon Jr., *Cast Iron Architecture in New York: A Photographic Survey* (Dover Publications, 1974), viii.

14. Gayle and Gillon, ix.

15. Johnson in Gayle and Gayle, 7.

Old Forms
New Materials

1. Frampton, 11.

2. Tarde, 128, (author's translation).

3. All Skene Catling quotations from Author's interview with Charlotte Skene Catling, 06/20/2019.

4. Quoted in "Ainu architecture: The "Chise" in *Heritage of Japan: Discovering the Historical Context and Culture of the People of Japan* (source The Nippon Kichi), accessed on line 9/23/18

5. This and following statements by Kengo Kuma quoted in Amy Frearson, "Meme Meadows Experimental House by Kengo Kuma and Associates" *Dezeen*, 1/16/13.

6. George Kubler quoted in *Copy Paste*, 42.

7. All BBP Arkitecter quotations from author's interview with Ebbe Wæhrens, 5/22/2019.

8. Chris Hodson, "BBP A Modern Merchant's House, Copenhagen, Denmark," *Copperconcept/ Copper in Architecture*,

10/29/14.

9. Giovanna Crespi, Interview with Simone Boldrin, *Casabella* 874 (June 201): 78-79 (author's translation).

10. Author's interview with Dr. Stephan Reimann, 6/04/2019

11. Certificate of Appropriateness issued by the New York City Landmarks Preservation Commission, 4/10/08, referring to the public meeting of 1/15/08.

12. Author's interview with Morris Adjmi, 9/15/18.

13. Roland Barthes, "Reflections on Photography" in *Camera Lucida,* Richard Howard, trans. (The Noonday Press, 1981), 26-27.

14. Edoardo Tresoldi, "Cavatorta and the Basilica di Siponto," www.cavatortagroup.com, accessed 8/26/19

New Forms
Old Materials

1. Peter Smithson, "Clients' instruction," in Robin Middleton, "In Pursuit of Ordinariness: Garden Building Oxford," *Architectural Design* (February 1971): 78-84.

2. Middleton, 78-84.

3. Middleton, 78-84.

4. www.herzogdemeuron.com, accessed 8/31/19.

5. www.winereviewonline.com/christian_moueix_part_2.cfm, accessed 8/31/19.

6. www.herzogdemeuron.com, accessed 8/31/19.

7. An expanded version of this essay was published as "Het Klooster voor de Fraters van Tilburg in Vught: een complex geheel" in *Cumulus, Werk und Ideen van Marx & Steketee architecten* (SUN, 2010).

8. Statement by Dorte Mandrup, included in the exhibition "Irreplaceable Landscapes," Danish Architecture Center, Copenhagen, spring 2019.

9. UNESCO World Heritage Center web site (whc.unesco.org/en/list/1314), accessed 8/6/19.

10. Thatching wall panel, "Irreplaceable Landscapes."

11. Kristoffer Lindhardt Weiss, *Vadehavscentret Dorte Mandrup* (Strandberg Publishing, 2018), 22.

Mimesis
In Defense of Imitation

1. Elaine Sturtevant, an artist who copied, repeated, and reconstructed Andy Warhol's flowers in 1965, quoted in her obituary by Hans Ulrich Obrist, *The Guardian*, 5/19/14.

2. Antoine Chrysostome Quatremère de Quincy, *An Essay on The Nature, The End, and The Means of Imitation in The Fine Arts*, translated from the French by J.C. Kent (Smith, Elder and Co., Cornhill Booksellers to Their Majesties, 1837), 14.

3. All quotations from author's interview with Teresa Borsuk, Senior Adviser at Pollard Thomas Edwards Architects, 6/19/19.

4. Gerard Buenen, "Why a Farmhouse?" in *MVRDV: The Glass Farm–Biography of a Building* (nai010, 2014), 121.

5. "Glass Farm, MVRDV," *Architect*, July 2014, accessed 7/8/18.

6. www.mvrdv.nl/projects/glass-farm, accessed 7/15/18.

7. www.archdaily.com Crystal Houses/, 4/20/16; "MVRDV Replaces Traditional Façade with Bricks That Are Stronger Than Concrete," *Dezeen*, 4/20/16.

8. "Crystal Houses, Hosting New Tenant Hermès, Re-Opens with an Even More Transparent Facade," MVRDV press release, 6/27/19.

9. www.hawkinsbrown.com, accessed 8/18/19.

10. Pamela Buxton, Interview with Seth Brown, Hawkins/Brown partner, *onOffice – Architecture and Design at Work*, 11/2/18.

11. All quotations from author's interview with Thomas Corbasson, 6/14/19.

12. All quotations from author's interview with Bernard Desmoulin, 6/12/19.

Bibliography

Aalto, Alvar. "Sketches/Alvar Aalto: The Humanizing of Architecture," *Sketches/Alvar Aalto*. Cambridge, Mass.: MIT Press, 1985, 77.

___. "E.G. Asplund In Memoriam" in Göran Schildt, ed., *Alvar Aalto In His Own Words*. New York: Rizzoli International Publications, 1997, 242-43.

Again, the Metaphor Problem and Other Engaged Critical Discourses about Art: A Conversation Between John Baldessari, Liam Gillick and Lawrence Weiner, Moderated by Beatrix Ruf. Vienna and New York: Springer, 2007.

"The Art of Copying, Ten Masters of Appropriation." *Artsy*, 02/11/ 2014.

Bachelard, Gaston. *The Poetics of Space*. New York: Orion Press, 1964.

Badger, Daniel D. *Badger's Illustrated Catalogue of Cast Iron Architecture*. New York: Dover Publications, 1981

Baldini, Umberto. *Santa Maria Novella: La Basilica, Il Convento, I Chiostri Monumentali*. Florence: Banca Toscana, 1981.

Beyst, Stefan. "Mimesis and Abstraction." *http://d-sites.net/english/abstraction.html*, 2005.

___. "Mimesis and Art." http://d-sites.net/ english/mimesisart.html, 2005.

Birksted, Jan Kenneth. "The Politics of Copying: Le Corbusier Immaculate Conceptions." *Oxford Art Journal* (6/1/2007): 305-26.

Bowley, Marian. *Innovations in Building Materials: An Economic Study*. London: Duckworth, 1960, 274-322.

Burisch, Nicole, Heather Anderson, Andrea Black. *Making Otherwise: Craft and Material Fluency in Contemporary Art*. Ottawa: Carleton University Art Gallery, 2018.

Burton, Johanna, and Anna Ellegood. *Take It or Leave It: Institution, Image, Ideology*. Los Angeles: Hammer Museum, 2014.

Candea, Matei, ed. *The Social after Gabriel Tarde: Debates and Assessments*. New York: Routledge, 2010.

Carpo, Mario. "Post Digital 'Quitters': Why the Shift Toward Collage Is Worrying." *Metropolis* (3/26/2018).

Cormier, Brendan, and Danielle Thom, eds. *A World of Fragile Parts: From the Special Project Organized by la Biennale di Venezia and the Victoria and Albert Museum*. London: V&A Publishing, 2016.

Cormier, Brendan. *COPY CULTURE: Sharing in the Age of Digital Reproduction*. London: V&A Publishing, 2018.

Deamer, Peggy, and Philip Bernstein, eds. *Building in the Future: Recasting Labor in Architecture*. New York: Princeton Architectural Press, 2010.

De Caigny, Sofie, et al. *Maatwerk—Made to Measure: Concept and Craft in Architectural Form from Flanders and the Netherlands*. Antwerp: Flanders Architecture Institute, 2016.

Dehaene, Michiel, Els Vervloesem, Marleen Goethals, Hüsnü Yegenoglu, eds. *Social Poetics—The Architecture of Use and Appropriation*. Rotterdam: OASE#96, 2016.

DeLanda, M. "Material Expressivity." *Domus* 893: 43.

de Quincy, Quatremère, *An Essay on the Nature, the End, the Means of Imitation in the Fine Arts*, J. C. Kent, trans. London: Smith, Elder and Co., Cornhill, 1837.

Denslagen, Wim, and Niels Gutschow eds. *Architectural Imitations: Reproductions and Pastiches in East and West*. Maastricht: Shaker Publishing BV, 2005.

Dovey, Kim. *Framing Places, Mediating Power in Built Form*. London: Routledge, 2002.

Drazin, Adam, and Susanne Küchler, eds. *The Social Life of Materials: Studies on Materials and Society*. London: Bloomsbury Academic, 2015.

Duro, Paul. "Why Imitation and Why Global?" Association of Art Historians, 2014.

von Engelberg-Dočkal, Eva. *Mimesis Bauen: Architektengespräche*. Paderborn: Brill/ Wilhelm Fink, 2017.

Fisher, Tom H. "What We Touch Touches Us: Materials, Affects, and Affordances." *Design Issues*, MIT Press, (Autumn 2004, 20.4): 20-31.

Frampton, Kenneth. *Studies in Tectonic Culture: The Poetics of Construction in Nineteenth and Twentieth Century Architecture*. Cambridge Mass.: MIT Press, 1995.

Fraser, Andrea. "From the Critique of Institutions to an Institution of Critique." *Artforum* 44 (9/2005): 278-83.

Fried, Michael. "Antiquity Now: Reading Winckelman on Imitation." *October* 37 (Summer 1986): 87-97.

Friedersdorf, Conor. "What Does 'Cultural Appropriation' Really Mean?" *The Atlantic* (4/3/2017).

Galchen, Rivka, and Anna Holmes. "What Distinguishes Cultural Exchange from Cultural Appropriation?" *New York Times* (6/8/2017).

Gayle, Margot. *Cast Iron Architecture in America: The Significance of James Bogardus*. New York: W. W. Norton, 1998.

Gentner, Derdre, and Brian Bowdle. "Metaphor as Structure-Mapping" in Raymond W. Gibbs, ed. *Handbook of Metaphor and Thought*. Cambridge: Cambridge University Press, 2008, 109-28.

Giovannini, Joseph. "Architectural Imitation: Is it Plagiarism?" *New York Times*, 3/17/1983.

Gould, Glenn. "Forgery and Imitation in the Creative Process." *Grand Street* 40 (Autumn 1994): 53-62.

Gutierrez Marquez, José Mario. "Collecting Metaphors," *Mediaesthetics, Zeitschrift für Poetologien Audiovisueller Bilder*, 2017

Hale, William Harlan. "Art Versus Yale University." *The Harkness Hoot* 1.2 (11/15/1930): 17-33.

Herzog and de Meuron 2005–2010. Madrid: El Croquis Editorial, 2010.

Kolarevic, Branko, and Kevin R. Klinger, eds. *Manufacturing Material Effects: Rethinking Design and Making in Architecture*. New York: Routledge, 2008.

Krauss, Rosalind. "The Future of an Illusion." *AA Files* (13.X Special Issue), 2018.

Kubler, George. *The Shape of Time: Remarks on the History of Things*. New Haven: Yale University Press, 1962.

Latour, Alessandra, ed. *Louis I. Kahn: Writings, Lectures, Interviews*. New York: Rizzoli International Publications, 1991.

Lees, Loretta. "Towards a Critical Geography of Architecture: The Case of an Ersatz Colosseu." *ECUMENE* (2001: 8): 51-86.

Lethem, Jonathan. "The Ecstasy of Influence: A Plagiarism by Jonathan Lethem." *Harper's Magazine*, 2007.

Lynch, Patrick. *Mimesis: Lynch Architects*. London: Artifice Books on Architecture, 2015.

MacKay-Lyons, Brian. *Local Architecture: Building, Place, Craft, and Community*. New York: Princeton Architectural Press, 2015.

Maas, Winy, Felix Madrazo, Diana Ibañez Lopez. *Copy Paste: The Badass Architectural Copy Guide*. Amsterdam: Why Factory and nai010 Publishers, 2017.

Mayernik, David. *The Challenge of Emulation in Art and Architecture*. Surrey, England, Burlington, VT.: Ashgate Publishing Co., 2013.

McCallum, I. "Syntax: The Contribution of the Curtain Wall to a New Vernacular." *Architectural Review* 121 (1957): 299-336.

Murray, Scott. *Contemporary Curtain Wall Architecture*. New York: Princeton Architectural Press, 2009.

Pallasmaa, Juhani. *The Eyes of The Skin: Architecture and the Senses*. Chichester, UK: John Wiley and Sons, 2012.

Porphyrios, Demetri. "Imitation and Convention." *Architectural Design* 58 (1/1/1988): 14.

Potts, Alex. "The Image Valued 'As Found' and the Reconfiguration of Mimesis in Post-War Art." *Art History*, Wiley Online Library, 2014.

Reynolds, Donald Martin. *Nineteenth Century Architecture*. Cambridge and New York: Cambridge University Press, 1992.

Riedijk, Michiel, ed. *Architecture as a Craft: Architecture, Drawing, Model, and Position*. Amsterdam: SUN Architecture Publishers, 2010

"7 Buildings that Marry Traditional Materials with Modern Forms." *Architizer*, 01/11/2020.

Smith, Samuel P. *Starting from "I don't know": Interviews on Architecture and Craft*. Chicago: Soberscove Press, 2015.

Stein, Amelia. "Does Architecture Need to Be Original?" *The Guardian*, 11/20/2015.

Tarde, Gabriel. *The Laws of Imitation*, Elsie Worthington Clews trans. New York: H. Holt & Company, 1903.

Tilley, Christopher. *Metaphor and Material Culture*. Oxford: Blackwell, 1999.

Weizman, Ines. "Architecture and Copyright: Loos, Law, and the Culture of the Copy." *ACSA 101, New Constellations, New Ecologies*,

 https://www.acsa-arch.org/proceedings/Annual%20Meeting%20Proceedings/ACSA.AM.101/ACSA.AM.101.112.pdf

Welchman, John C. *Art After Appropriation: Essays on Art in the 1990s*. Amsterdam: G+B Arts International, 2001.

Acknowledgments

Material Transfers is the result of several years of reflection and ruminations: conversations with friends and colleagues—architects, historians, colleagues at Columbia University—have contributed to its development, and I am grateful for their input. First and foremost, I want to thank Ken Frampton, who saw the material early on and, in a couple of conversations, made critical comments that resulted in a better focus on the significant aspects of this work. I would also like to thank Harry Kendall and Jayne Merkel for reading the text and making useful comments, as well as Jorge Otero-Pailos for our conversation on a preliminary building selection.

The pleasure of seeing the buildings and meeting with their architects and owners is one of the great joys of working on such a project, and I am grateful to those who were generous with their time and their ideas: Morris Adjmi and Micheal Zweck-Bronner in New York, Ebbe Waehrens in Copenhagen, Anna Reimann and Dr. Stephan Reimann in Kantzem an der Saar, Teresa Borsuk in London, Charlotte Skene Catling in London, Niall Hobhouse in Somerset, Thomas Corbasson in Paris, and Bernard Desmoulin in Paris.

I would also like to thank the architects and photographers who allowed me to use their material for publication: Kengo Kuma and Associates, BBP Arkitekter, Max Dudler, Jimi Billingsley, Ximo Michavilla, Dorte Mandrup, Pollard Thomas Edwards Architects, MVRDV, Chartier Corbasson Architectes, and Bernard Desmoulin Architecte.

This book would not be what it is without its editor, Elizabeth White, whose fine sense of its focus is so critical to its cohesion. I also want to thank Shawn Hazen of Hazen Creative for his excellent graphic design.

Lastly, I want to acknowledge the role Tom Killian has played in this work: first and ultimate reader and constant commentator; this is dedicated to him.